T0064537

DAY-TO-DAY WRITINGS
FROM
JESUS OF NAZARETH
THROUGH
JAMES COYLE MORGAN

BALBOA.
PRESS
A DIVISION OF HAY HOUSE

Copyright © 2015 Sandra A. Schrock.

All rights reserved. No part of this book may be used or reproduced by any means, graphic, electronic, or mechanical, including photocopying, recording, taping or by any information storage retrieval system without the written permission of the publisher except in the case of brief quotations embodied in critical articles and reviews.

Balboa Press books may be ordered through booksellers or by contacting:

Balboa Press
A Division of Hay House
1663 Liberty Drive
Bloomington, IN 47403
www.balboapress.com
1 (877) 407-4847

Because of the dynamic nature of the Internet, any web addresses or links contained in this book may have changed since publication and may no longer be valid. The views expressed in this work are solely those of the author and do not necessarily reflect the views of the publisher, and the publisher hereby disclaims any responsibility for them.

The author of this book does not dispense medical advice or prescribe the use of any technique as a form of treatment for physical, emotional, or medical problems without the advice of a physician, either directly or indirectly. The intent of the author is only to offer information of a general nature to help you in your quest for emotional and spiritual well-being. In the event you use any of the information in this book for yourself, which is your constitutional right, the author and the publisher assume no responsibility for your actions.

Any people depicted in stock imagery provided by Thinkstock are models, and such images are being used for illustrative purposes only.
Certain stock imagery © Thinkstock.

Print information available on the last page.

ISBN: 978-1-5043-3526-3 (sc)
ISBN: 978-1-5043-3527-0 (e)

Library of Congress Control Number: 2015910203

Balboa Press rev. date: 8/18/2015

FOREWORD

The following material came into being through my, now, late step father James Coyle Morgan in conjunction with the writing of two manuscripts, "Jesus and Mastership" and "The New Book of Revelation," while he and my mother were ministering in Fresno, California, in the Unity Church.

During that time, James and my mother, Audré would occasionally ponder the messages Jesus had given, and this in turn caused them to want more information on various topics. So, the next time James sat down to write on the manuscript, Jesus would respond to their questions, which you will find here in these "Day To Day Writings".

My mother and step father were grateful beyond words for the experience bestowed upon them and feel that whoever reads this text will also be wonderfully blessed.

This manuscript "Day To Day Writings" with Jesus which was channeled through James, has meant so much to my parents and myself that I want to share this with you the reader. This manuscript was written in my life time so it makes me feel close to Jesus and his words of wisdom almost as if I had lived on earth at the same time as Jesus did and was able to know and work with him, what a wonderful honor that would have been. "Day To Day Writings" has been a blessing to me, so I want to pass the blessing on to you.

The picture of Jesus in the book was painted by me, with the help of Jesus and maybe others on the spirit side. Jesus was painted with LOVE to be a blessing.

GOD BLESS YOU

Sandra Schrock

JESUS' DISCOURSES WITH JAMES COYLE MORGAN
1970 - 1971

Question: "How do you praise God?"

I (Jesus) would like to comment on Praise, which is a form of prayer, as you know. Praise is a necessary ingredient to building or forming a happy, successful life. Praise multiplies all it touches, and increases your good as you use it wisely in your daily living. Praise, coupled with thanksgiving develops a power to produce good that is second to none. A sincere "Thank You," given prior to asking God for that which you desire, is a sure sign you will receive your wish, as this shows your faith and also constitutes a form of praise.

There is only one way to truly praise God, and that is to do everything you can to make yourself and your life as perfect as the Father sees you. This in itself is the highest praise you can give God, as it shows your acceptance of God laws and guidance to be the best you know, or you would not try to "copy" God life. Imitation and copying after are high forms of praise. To endeavor to express the Christ within you, shows that you approve of and commend to others the work of God. As you do this, your life will be doubly enriched.

Praise and thanksgiving shows your appreciation of that, which you praise and give thanks for. Without praise and thanksgiving, life would be flat, dull, and lifeless. So praise God by endeavoring to perfect yourself in all things God teaches.

Question: Regarding the statement "You Cannot Serve God and Mammon," which has brought much comment and some confusion.

Indeed, you cannot think of God nor serve God if all your thinking and working time is spent trying to make money, or thinking of things and ways to satisfy your sensual desires and vanity. You cannot serve two masters, for you will give all you have to one and neglect the other.

Those who moonlight or take second jobs, usually do so for the sake of the money they get out of it. Therefore, they do as little as possible on the job. Only enough to get by; or in other words "lip service."

Many people give "lip service" to Truth also, as their true interests lie somewhere else. My message to all is to stop worry and concern about material things; that is, health, happiness and/ or what others do or have. Stop fighting the world to obtain what you want and need. Instead, relax and let God guide you in your actions, just as the birds are guided in feeding themselves with the food that is provided from the ample supply of God.

Question: Do you have any comment on Keeler's statements regarding the Master State of Mind, and that we heal by Christian knowing?

Yes, his (Keeler's) statements are essentially correct. I did say, "The Kingdom of God is Within," and was referring to it as being a state of mind. I was thinking of and meaning, that this is a state of mind analogous to the Christ Mind or Divine Mind in reality. It is a state of mind, that is directed by and in tune with the Christ Mind or Divine Mind. This can be achieved, as you have done and are doing, by giving yourself to God in prayer and meditation and by practicing the presence of God, as in these classes, as well as in your daily prayer work and activities. In reality, it is a Christ-like state of mind in many respects. It is part of the Christ Mind, but not all of it. The subliminal state of mind, is a state reached consciously that is a very high state of mind spiritually. It is an inner knowing of spiritual things. It is between the conscious and subconscious, and actually is of the superconscious phase of mind. It is difficult to try to explain a feeling and knowing that is spiritually right, and that actually is the activity of God at work through you as a channel, fulfilling and healing all that is brought within it. It is in this state of mind that I (Jesus) healed or was a channel for the healing power to flow through. And right now, Jim, you are in this state of mind. Many times as you and Audré teach and talk or counsel with others, you are entering this state of mind. You might say it is a state of mind in which the intuition, the conscious, subconscious, and the superconscious phases of mind meet as one, and are directed as the Spirit of God directs.

So, in a state of mind like that, healing does take place. Keeler's explanation of the healing process is a good one, but of course of itself it does not heal. There must be a clear channel through which God's Spirit can flow in order to heal.

All healing is done by the Spirit of God. God life in all people and living creatures responds to the Spirit of God; thus dissolving all conditions that do not express the perfection of God ideas, so the healing can occur.

Question: Brother, what action takes place in the body when it is being healed?

That is a good question and one that can help change the thinking of those that hear the answer. Of course, the first thing that takes place is the removal of the cause. In other words, the thought or emotion that initially formed the ailment by slowing down the flow of life-giving God love.

Then, the Spirit begins to dissolve the negative condition, and the new cells that are being continuously manufactured start to rebuild the body and organs that have been weakened by the onslaught of disease. Naturally, there is a chemical reaction that takes place, which changes from the diseased or damaged condition to one of healing and rebuilding. The Spirit takes care of this reaction. In fact, Spirit brings it about and controls it.

The beauty of God life flowing through the body heals and strengthens it, just as my (Jesus') body was healed through the action of God life flowing in and through it. The Spirit first guided certain cells to more or less function like a surgeon's knife, and remove the damaged flesh. Then other cells began rebuilding the places that had been damaged, until the healing was completed. Sometimes this can be done almost instantly, or over a period of time, depending on the state of mind or attitude of the individual.

In the case of my (Jesus') body in the tomb, we, Elijah, Moses, and myself, were also completing the spiritualization of the body, thus it reguired a little more time as the Spirit's realizing process can cause some damage to the body if it is too fast, because of the tremendous power that is being used. It is somewhat like the use of electricity in the wiring of your house through appliances to achieve a certain effect; or a ball of lightning, which is the same power, but uncontrolled, so it damages rather than rebuilds.

Question: Have all souls been created? Or are they still being created?

All souls have been created that will be created in the universe.

Question: Concerning transmigration and whether the human soul was ever in animal.

No, it is human at the time of creation. All animals have animal souls and remain animals. They were never intended to be anything else.

Animals may at some time be extinct as such and some other form of life may replace them. Animals were not placed on the earthplane to be **eaten** by man, but man started eating them and will in the future learn to do without meat in any form. It does not help man to eat meat.

Question: Why do some people look and act like animals?

That is more or less correct. Some individuals have associated with animals so much, that they take on the characteristics of animals. Others have supressed their spiritual nature and let their animal or material nature have full control of their minds and bodies; hence the animal characteristics and actions.

Question: Do you have any comments on wisdom?

Yes, by all means one should use wisdom in all he/she does. Only the ignorant individual goes forth without first planning his/her course and looking for the best way to accomplish that which he/she desires to do. Simple pleasures are good to help one relax, but when indulged in to an excess can be injurious to one's progress. Wisdom should be used in all of one's activities whether eating, sleeping, working, playing, creating, meditating, or any other activity. An excess of any one thing brings an imbalance into one's life, and when there is an imbalance (too much of one thing), there is a lack of some needed thing.

Question: Do you have any comment regarding the lesson subject "Life?"

Yes, I do. The life of God which is also represented by wine in manifest forms, both visible and invisible, is formed and unformed throughout the universe. Life is God. God is life and is everywhere present in the universe and proven by science. Religion has been saying this for many years. It is just another way science and religion are drawing closer together in beliefs. The Tree of Life, in the Garden of Eden, with its roots in the good earth or material part of life and its trunk and branches reaching to the heights of spiritual glory in God, is thus uniting the material and the Spirit in one body or unit that expresses God in all its glory. Man is to do the same. His feet on the ground, that is, his understanding of materialistic tendencies, and his body upright. The spine and nervous system, (the trunk and branches of the tree reaching to the heights of God glory at the peak of the brain), are to be combined to manifest Conscious Oneness with God as man spiritualizes his body, raising it to new glory in God.

However, many who may be turning their attention from God to material or sensual things, lose their spiritual understanding and deprive themselves of their good. That is the same as being thrown out of the Garden of Eden. Life, when treated with respect and wisdom will bring unalloyed happiness to the individual.

Question: Relevance of Speaking in Tongues?

Speaking in tongues is a good spiritual experience for some, but **can** lead to rather difficult experiences with entities, that are more or less earthbound. This can be temporary, but can also become permanent. I do not recommend this to anyone. Actually, speaking in tongues does no one any real good, as nobody really knows what is said.

Question: What was the custom in the synagogue, since in the Bible it says: "When it came my turn to speak."

In the synagogue each man took his turn to read the scripture and then make whatever remarks he chose about that portion of which he read. The books of the Bible are separate books in the synagogue, not one large book such as the standard Bible. Some of the books do have different names also.

Question: How can or does the Father surrender Himself to man?

The word surrender may be the incorrect word to use. However, man surrenders or submits himself to God the Father. The Father accepts the gift and enfolds the individual in His all embracing Spirit. So the word or phrase should read, "This can be achieved in no other way than in complete submission of oneself to me, as I enfold him in my all embracing Spirit." Yes, submission is a better word to use than surrender, because in submitting you yield your mind and will to God's will, and let God guide you in the decisions of how you will think, speak and all.

Question: Do you have any comment to make on our lesson on Power?

Yes, Power is what makes the universe move and expand in divine order. God is power. Power is God; spiritual power.

I used spiritual power when I fed the multitudes. The power used converted substance into the food the people ate. I used spiritual power when I raised Lazarus from the dead. Everyone is using spiritual power in their daily life as they go about their daily affairs. The spiritual power is used to think, to speak, and to act. These actions produce results in their activities. We all have spiritual power and direct it as we wish. We can tell how we are directing it or using it by the results we find in viewing our circumstances and conditions, under which we are living.

One of the most important ways we use spiritual power is through our speech. The words convey the thought, but the thought continued in the words is enhanced and strengthened by the power of faith and belief in that which is being spoken, by letting the power of the Father flow through us.

It was said that "I spoke with authority," because I knew that what I was saying was the Truth. I believed it, and the Father gave power to my words. You have power and you will speak with power and authority tomorrow.

Question: Brother, is it right for medical science to do everything it can to keep an elderly person alive, when he/she is mentally and physically deteriorating and seems to be in a more or less vegetative state, lying in bed, awaiting the release of death?

Jim, this is a question that has been asked many, many times. I think the soul is clinging to a life, hoping for something better, and is in fear of releasing itself to freedom from limitation in a spent or deteriorated body. Actually, nothing is really gained by holding on to life on the earthplane in such a body, when the spiritual understanding of the soul has not risen to the place of spiritualizing the body.

Life, when it is being lived as you have seen in some of those elderly people in convalescent homes, is not very pleasant. It would seem as though the soul would release itself, but in many cases it is either trying to learn something or trying to teach a lesson to someone else. I do not think medical science should be overly anxious to prolong life in a badly deteriorated body, just for the sake of their desire to extend life.

Question: Would you care to comment on how zeal is to be used in achieving spiritual growth in oneself and in helping others?

Yes, I would like to discuss zeal. Zeal is a necessary ingredient to achieve the heights of glory in God, as zeal or enthusiasm is the motivating force behind all activity. When one enters into any activity with enthusiasm, one gets things done because one releases an energy that has been stored within oneself awaiting release. The release of energy is triggered because there is a desire to accomplish some goal, as soon, or as quickly as possible. This desire is coupled with enthusiasm or zeal, which is the driving force behind all of man's activities, directed toward attaining some goal. Zeal is a sustaining force supported by faith, that the goal can be attained.

Zeal, supported by faith becomes a great driving power in man, that can bring forth the ability as well as capability to achieve any goal. Wisdom is added to this powerful force to guide it in the direction it must go.

Men/women with a desire to accumulate great wealth and power, have used the driving force of zeal and faith, and directed it with wisdom to achieve their goal. And after having accumulated great wealth and attained much power, only to pass away, leaving behind the wealth and power to go on with a soul starved for spiritual understanding of God. Great wars have been fought and countless people killed because of someone's driving ambition to achieve power. This is misusing God-given powers to accomplish selfish ends and becomes self-destructive.

Zeal is a power given to us to add flavor to our lives, just as salt adds flavor to food, when used with wisdom and tempered by love and understanding.

It was in this manner, that I was able to accomplish all that which I did. I started out with a desire to help mankind rise above its bondage to fear and materialistic tendencies, and find instead the good life in God.

I had faith that the Spirit of God would flow through me, leading and guiding me in what I was to do. The desire to help mankind released the zeal and enthusiasm I needed. The zeal, supported by faith was directed by the spiritual love, understanding and wisdom of God. I then submitted myself to God and let this force work through me. I was able to become the living example, demonstrating the Truth I taught.

Question: Brother, are the things written in the Lost Books of the Bible true about you and your youth?

Some of them are. However, I did not cause anyone harm or suffering as told in the Book. I did heal and strengthen people. It would have been against God to use my power to kill or harm anyone, and I would have destroyed myself if I had.

Question: Do you have any comment regarding understanding?

Understanding exists on two levels of mind action. Intellectual understanding is arrived at by use of the conscious phase of mind action, and is founded on information supplied by or from various sources. This is the basis on which many judge other's behavior, or their own, when they are going to take some action or create something.

Understanding the laws and their use provides a good existence for a human in this earth life.

The other level of mind on which understanding is arrived at, is from the superconscious phase of mind, and comes directly from the Spirit of God in man. It is a sense of knowing something without being sure just how one knows it. King Solomon's decision regarding the two mothers and the baby, is a good example of this. Knowing the real mother without having any actual facts on which to base his (Solomon) decision, except the knowledge of human nature, and the way mother love would react to the killing of the child. Man can develop his intuitive power by becoming open and receptive to Spirit, and thus follow his own guidance. You have covered this in your lesson. So this can be the summation of your lesson. God Bless You.

Question: What is Truth?

Truth is God for God is Truth. Truth is absolute. Truth is the Reality of God that does not change nor vary. The path of Truth is the path to expressing Conscious Oneness with God. Oneness with God can only be attained through the application of Truth principles to one's life, and using the divine laws in the right way. The only way is through **prayer** and **meditation.** Yes, Jim, you and Audré answered the question well. As the individual must of necessity find Truth for him/herself. Books and teachers can only be a guide. The true seeker must go within to find Truth, and when the seeker does, he/she finds God.

The thought you have, that the purpose of the book regarding my (Jesus') life, is to show all people that the process of spiritual growth in the individual, during this lifetime on the earth plane, is a step by step, do-it-yourself program. It begins with the unlimited potential within the individual when he/she enters this lifetime at birth; and becomes a continual day by day activity until his/her exit as a Master or soul separated from his/her body to try again. It is to show that I had to do the same thing, and that, at various times, I could have succumbed to temptation and not completed the demonstration I was to make. So many have set me on the pedestal of the incarnated God, and think that they themselves are worms of the dust, sinners not fit, etc. Thus, these people have no thought of doing the same as I did. This illusion must be destroyed, and new life and goals injected into the minds of all humanity. Yes, Jim and Audré, we have quite an objective before us. A worthy goal for true Masters, which we can accomplish by the power of God, flowing through us all.

The Word of God is the creative power of God in more or less concrete form. The spoken word of man directs the creative power in a definite direction, and stimulates the activity of the mind by the thought or meaning, conveyed by the word itself. This, in turn, stimulates emotions, and when emotion is involved with the creative power, action takes place. Emotion is stimulated by desire and desire stimulated by words. Words are the intellectual description of imaginative pictures in the mind or inner vision, which are creative in themselves. Thus, the creative power of God is invoked by the mind activity, and multiplied by the power of the spoken word. This is just a brief explanation about the power of the Word of God.

Question: Do you have any comments on the lesson of living purposefully?

The true purpose of every living soul is to express Conscious Oneness with God. This is done by developing one's spiritual awareness of God being within oneself and within everyone else. Such an awareness, in turn, helps the individual to treat him/herself kindly, as well as that of his/her fellow human. This is another way of stating the Golden Rule, **"Do unto others as you would have others do unto you."** You must first love and respect yourself before you can love and respect others. For you see in others what you see in yourself. See the Christ within yourself, and you will see the Christ in others. Through prayer and meditation one develops awareness of God, or the Son of God, Christ within oneself. The awareness and spiritual understanding has to come from within. If you are not happy, well, strong and/or prosperous, but desire more of these conditions, then **STOP.**

Look (within and at yourself), and then go within in prayer and ask God for help. Then, listen for the guidance, that is, "letting go and letting God" take charge of your life. This will be the greatest move you have ever made.

Question: Is it true that most of your disciples studied with the Essenes?

Yes, it is true that most of them did. I did not meet them, however, as I had not been to the part of the country where they lived and studied since my return from the East. The Essenes believed in the One God, but not quite in the same manner as I came to believe and teach. They did believe they could worship God in other places than the Temple in Jerusalem, although, that was the best place to go to get closer to Him.

Question: Do you care to comment on the lesson: "Love is a Magnet for Sunday?"

Yes. As you know, I think love is the most important part of mankind's relationship with each other. I said, that the greatest commandment is to love God with all your mind, heart, and soul. And the second is to love your neighbor as yourself. By this I meant that every individual is to submit himself to God and put God first in his life. It is most difficult to love an intangible God. However, God is Love, and Love is God. Therefore, if one loves and respects himself, one is loving God and letting God express through him. When a person loves and respects himself, he likewise loves and respects a fellow human. No individual can truly love another person, unless loving him/herself first. (If this is difficult, love the Christ within yourself as well as in others).

The reason why many marriages fail is, because one, the other, or both individuals involved do not truly love each other. Instead, they are trying to fulfill a selfish desire to satisfy their longing for love without really considering the other person. They do not love or respect themselves, or they would give of themselves rather than merely taking from the other.

True love gives without expecting return and, yet, acts as a magnet that draws love to itself. True love is inspiring, strengthening, healing, guiding, and, powerful. It builds and supports that which is loved. Personal love or passion is selfish and debilitating. It tears down and is destructive. It feeds on itself and becomes self-destructive. Thus, it is only temporary and burns itself out. True love increases and grows with the passing of time. True Love is God expressing through humankind. And in return, humanity loves God.

I did teach, that we should feel a oneness with each other, instead of fearing one another. I realize it is difficult to express love for many in the present time of dissention, riots and crime of all sorts. But when the individual lets the Power of God Love flow through his/her mind and heart, that person is protected from all harm. A person must hold to the Truth, that God Love is a protecting, stengthening, and healing power in which an individual lives, moves, and has his/her being. One is never separated from that love, as one is always in the presence of God. But each must become conscious of that love, and let it flow through their being.

I did teach that we should let God guide us in the procurement of our necessities of life. When we follow our guidance, we obtain an abundant supply of everything easily without stress or strain.

Question: Can God speak to us when we are in tune, and if there is a need to be taken care of?

God does not and cannot speak as such. God doesn't do anything -- God is; just as Divine Mind is. Your own individual part of Divine Mind does not do anything as such. Thoughts and ideas are in Divine Mind to which the individual has access. Thoughts and ideas are indicative of the action that the Spirit of God, which is the activity of God, takes in and through the individual mind of God. The activity of God or Divine Mind is activity of Spirit in man.

As for man hearing the voice of God, it could not be, as God does not have a voice as such. However, Masters have been known to speak to men to guide them in some manner for their own good. Entities have been known to speak to the individual, but not always for the individuals highest good.

God speaks through thoughts and feelings, not through an inner voice. This would limit God. God **is** Spirit. Therefore, acts and speaks as Spirit, not as a limited being with a voice.

Yes, the still small voice is not a sound, but a feeling engendered by the Spirit. Likely you have heard the voice of a Master speaking to you trying to help you. This you will also do for mankind, after you become Masters.

Jim, you wonder how I can spend so much time with the two of you when there are so many millions calling on me. There is no simple answer to satisfy you except to say, that I can instantly respond to any person's needs. I do not necessarily have to leave here to respond to others. Besides, there are several other Masters who also work with me to help those who call. They (Masters) can do the same as I do. Furthermore, **this project is now the most important work we are doing, as the whole of mankind is entering into a new phase of their existence and life, on the earth plane.** And as we have said before, you two lovely people are a special part of it. In fact, the most important part at this time. And as time goes on, your part will become even more important to the successful outworking of our plan.

Others who call are taken care of by the Father working through us and the individual who is calling. In a sense, I am a focal point for them to concentrate on in order to open themselves to the in-flowing Spirit of God, which does the real work of fulfilling their desires and needs. So you see, we can spend all the time we think is required with you. Assisting you in all you do, and helping you to grow and unfold spiritually. Thus enabling you to do more effective work there on the earth plane. This also is preparing the two of you to become Masters just that much sooner. This may give you some answer to your question, Jim. As you continue on, you will understand more. I see you have a glimmering of an idea how we work.

Question: Do you have any comments to make regarding our lesson for tomorrow: "The Altar?"

Yes, the Altar is the "abiding place of the Most High," deep within one's soul. It is a definite place where only the individual can go to commune with God. No one else can go in there. It is a sacred place; the meeting place between God and man.

The truth is that one can not really enter this secret place until one has relinquished all feelings of unforgiveness for others. Feelings of resentment, criticism, hate, envy, jealousy, greed, and fear block the path to the inner Altar or place of peaceful communion with God, the Father. When one has released these feelings they return to the state of nothingness from which they came. One should also forgive oneself and seek forgiveness of others one has harmed in some manner. Through prayer one can do this. There can be true communion with God when all negative feelings are released. Through this communion, love and peace fill the mind and heart, and are expressed to all mankind. This is God expressing through man. If man continues to express criticism, resentment, hate, and unforgiveness toward others, he becomes a prisoner of such negative feelings and is held in bondage to them until such a time when he releases them. In the meantime, the person suffers the consequences of his/her feelings, through sickness, lack and insecurity.

Question: Brother, are twin souls and soul mates the same?

No, twin souls refer to those souls that are close together, such as so-called brothers and sisters or father and mother. While soul mates are those two souls, that when brought together compliment each other to such an extent, that they make a perfect pair to become one; such as Father-Mother God.

There is only one soul that is the identity of each individual. And each soul has always been or existed, as there is no beginning or end of the soul in-as-much as each soul houses the **I AM** or Christ Self of the individual.

Soul mates develop through the ages as they come together many times and live together both embodied and in the etheric plane, until they become the true complimentary soul of the other, or one spiritually.

Question: Immaculate Conception?

There have been many immaculate conceptions in the earth life plane through the ages. As Audre says, on some planets babies are conceived mentally in the female body. There is no physical intercourse, as such, to conceive children; only mental.

Question: What is meant by the passage in John 14:1-4, regarding the Father's house and many rooms?

This is something I am supposed to have said to the disciples, which in the translations have been changed from that which was actually said. I told the disciples that I was going to go ahead of them and would return to tell them of the life where I was going. As you now know, I only knew there was a place for spiritualized man, but did not know much about it. I told what I did to encourage the men and give them something to hold onto, until I could actually describe in detail the way of life after spiritualizing and raising the body. We all knew about life in the astral and etheric planes, but also suspected there was something else.

Question: The Sabbath?

Yes, entering the Sabbath, which is not just prayer, but action as well, can lead one to one's highest good. In the silence of the Sabbath one receives guidance on what one is to think, say and do. A person also receives wisdom, knowledge, and understanding with which to control his/her actions and reactions as well as emotional feelings, desires and impulses. An individual thus, has dominion over his/her thoughts and can direct them into the right channels to bring into manifestation his/her unlimited good. It is only through the guidance of the Father, that a person can achieve his/her highest goal, which is Conscious Oneness with God. This guidance comes in the silence of one's soul while observing the true Sabbath, in complete submission, love, and obedience to God, the Father.

Question: Eating of meat?

Actually, the eating of meat is not for the highest good of anyone, as you well know. Although, to most people this habit is not injurious. However, the vibrations contained in the meat is not conducive to spiritual growth, because of the animal content. The killing of animals for meat is, by far, the most harmful to humans. Such activity is contrary to all spiritual laws and should be stopped. I do not know, however, that meat eating has anything to do with the cause of large death tolls in natural catastrophes. But the killing of animals definitely prevents mankind from rising above danger. Therefore, this can be a cause of large death tolls. The killing of animals leads to the killing of humans. I do not think you are in a position, at the present time, to say much about the subject as it would do little good. However, after you have gained prominence in the project, you can mention this, and it will bear more weight and have some effect. Actually, in time it (eating of meat) will be eliminated from the lives of mankind.

Question: Do you wish to say something concerning overcoming?

An "Overcomer" is one who rises above all temptations and challenges, just as I did. I was an "Overcomer." The "Overcomer" does not resist challenges and temptations, but takes appropriate action to dissolve them. While in the wilderness, after my baptism, I dissolved the final temptations by eliminating my desire for them through the action of letting the Spirit of God fill my mind and heart with the love and fullness of God. Thus, anything less was no longer a temptation. Each challenge or so-called "problem," that loomed in my way to my ultimate goal, was dissolved by the action of the Spirit of God, working through the situation and bringing it to a conclusion in divine order.

Question: Are the young people that Armstrong was speaking of, sincere in turning to you or is it a put on? Did you have long hair, as shown in the picture of you, etc?

The young people, the hippies, that are discovering a Jesus Christ of the Bible, are sincerely seeking me; just as Armstrong is. But both have different ideas regarding me. The teaching, as given in my story, is the true one. But the Bible version is not exactly so, as you know. I think these young people will more readily accept the version in my story, than will Armstrong and others like him. That is why I am so desirous in getting the book "Jesus and Mastership" published.

And yes, I did wear long hair and still do. I also wear clothes about the same as shown in various pictures, as that was the style of clothing worn then and still is, in some countries, in the East. That type of clothing is more comfortable than what you wear now.

Question: Does killing in a war action become a karmic debt for those that do the killing? What about (Lt.) Calley (in Viet Nam)?

Yes, killing, for any reason, becomes a karmic debt on the individual. War or no war, the killing of men, women and children, which Calley and his men did in the village, was no more reprehensible than any other killing.

The Manson people also killed and feel they did no wrong; just as Calley feels he was right. These individuals will have to settle their karmic debt before they can grow more spiritually. Probably the Manson group will be restrained from reincarnating until they learn better, which may take a long time.

The wartime killings are done in a different state of mind; therefore, will be atoned for much sooner, and the soul will return to work out their karmic debts.

Question: Would you comment on The Spiritual Communion?

Yes, we will begin with the entrance into Jerusalem, since that should come first in our lesson. Entering Jerusalem is symbolic of entering a peaceful state of mind. It is necessary for us to be at peace, if we are to receive the good we desire. For only when our minds and hearts are at peace, are we open and receptive to the love and wisdom of God. When we are uptight, angry, resentful, envious, greedy, nervous, and filled with other negative emotions, the channels through which God love and wisdom flow, become either restricted or stopped completely. This can be opened by prayer, and turning to God within; giving our thoughts to thoughts of God and His peace and love for all mankind.

In the individual, the Christ is the pattern that each one is to express in the outer. When we are open and receptive, the Christ love, which is God love in the individual, will freely flow in and through us; healing, strengthening and prospering us.

Question: Any comments on life between lives, and how many planes are there?

There are several planes on which souls exist. There is the earth plane in which the soul is in a body; and the astral plane in which the soul is held by its state of mind. It desires to return to the earth plane, but cannot, as it is not ready nor prepared to. It (soul) has to dissolve its desires, which can only be satisfied by a physical body.

The etheric plane is where the soul learns and expands in mental and spiritual ways. It grows and prepares to re-embody in order to grow more, and to complete itself through the addition of the spiritualized body.

The spiritualized earth plane is the place where the soul exists in a spiritualized body of a Master. It is expressing Conscious Oneness with God.

It has been said, by some students and in study courses or schools, that there are more planes of higher understanding. This is not true. Many souls go higher in Spiritual understanding on the etheric plane, but are not complete without the spiritualized body.

On the spiritualized plane, the Master can go wherever he/she desires in the universe and does. This then is the highest spiritual plane.

It all depends on the state of mind of the soul. The soul has the knowledge and the understanding, but it has to apply it through a physical body and rise above all limitations, mental and physical. Spiritualize the body and raise it, just as I did, in order to be in the spiritualized earth plane. The only way the soul can get to that plane, is in a spiritualized body. It is not an easy thing to do, but you, Jim and Audre, have almost done it. Keep up the way you are going, and you will be here with us eventually. We will be with you all the way, helping all we can.

Question: Brother, am I getting your thoughts regarding what you would like for me to bring to the people tomorrow out of your Life Story?

Yes Jim, you are very receptive and we are in accord about the Truth regarding my resurrection; and the Truth about every other soul's resurrection, which is the same. However, it is not necessary to experience the physical act of death. As I pointed out, in the account, it is easier to spiritualize and raise the body while it is still alive, than after it is dead. One very big reason is, that as soon as the soul separates itself from the body, life leaves the body and it begins to deteriorate very quickly. This is the natural process of returning to the substance from which the body was formed in the universe. Since the body begins immediately to return to its original substance (decompose), it is easier to heal and rebuild the body while life is still in it. That is why Moses and Elijah came to help me

(Jesus), as my body had been brutally treated, and then began to deteriorate when I removed the soul. Thus, there was almost double work that had to be done. However, I had almost completed the action by the time they (Moses and Elijah) appeared on the scene. It can be done (healing and rebuilding body), but the process is much more difficult (after departure of soul).

Question: Did you hear Audré's question about your ability to move things here in the apartment or anything else anywhere in the earth plane?

Yes, I heard her question. Indeed, we (Masters) can move anything we desire, especially if there is a good purpose for doing so. Peter (disciple) did strum the strings on Emmett's (Audré's son) guitar, just as I am moving your (Jim) arm to write. It (moving objects) takes time and effort, but can be done. If you desire, we (Masters) will give you a demonstration sometime soon.

Question: Any additional information on life between lives? Who does the teaching of entities on the etheric plane? Can you as a Master go to the etheric plane, as well as to the astral plane?

Yes, a Master can go to all planes, as he/she desires, as well as to any other place in the universe. A Master can go anywhere, in order to be of most service to mankind, which means serving God. The teachers on the etheric plane, are mostly highly evolved souls, who do not seem to have any desire to re-embody to become Masters. For one reason or another, they prefer to serve humankind by teaching souls to become better men and women.

The Ancient White Brotherhood consists of Masters who are devoting themselves to the same purpose. Souls do need training before they re-embody, which is why souls go from the astral plane to the etheric plane before re-embodying. Occasionally, an earth-bound soul will try to go back before going to the etheric plane, but is either stopped before the conception, or the baby is stillborn or the soul is separated from the body soon after birth. If it (baby) were to continue living, it would be a disastrous experience for the soul and everyone else connected with it. Since this has happened in the past, every effort is made to prevent such a thing from re-occurring. The events that follow are not good, in cases where some (earth-bound souls) have made it (re-embodied before going to the etheric plane). There is more that can be said, but this should suffice.

Question: Who inspired those who wrote the Scriptures you (Jesus) **quoted and who prophesied your crucifixion,** etc?

That is a good question. Actually, many of the so-called visions were inspired by Masters in the spiritualized earth plane, who had the inspiration and vision of the Father. However, Isaiah was inspired by spiritual revelations coming through his own Higher Self, his Christ Self. I respected his (Isaiah) revelations as being true, and thus quoted him more than others. All mankind and prophets have been impressed with spiritual revelations or thoughts by Masters such as I (Jesus). You were impressed by me, as well as your own spiritual revelations through the Father. Most of your spiritual revelations have come directly from the Father.

I have helped guide you (Jim) in the many steps and ways you have travelled since 1947, believe it or not! The same thing applies to Audré. Except, Miriam was and is working with her, in addition to that, which I have been doing with her (Audre) since 1946. How about that!

Question: Do you (Jesus) have any comments on "The Two Faces of Man?"

The face of personality that a person shows to the world in an effort to cover up thoughts and feelings is really transparent. That which an individual is thinking comes through unwittingly, and without the individual realizing it. Thus, a person fools no one except him/herself.

In this day and age, the image that others have of a person has become of primary importance to those in the public eye, and to businesses. The so-called image shown to the public, is the personality and can be made to appear as desired by the individual, or business. However, the inner thoughts, feelings and emotions eventually filter through the facade, and the image projected becomes false. Therefore, it behooves each person to go within to the true inner Self, the Christ Self or the I AM, which is the individuality; the true face that each person is to show to the world. This is the True Self that God expresses through in manifesting Himself to the outer world. Man is the channel through which God expresses. The more open the channel, the more God expresses. This then is the face a person is to show to the world. The individuality face will eventually show through the personality face, and becomes the face we are to show the world. An unchanging, loving, beautiful face expressing the love of God for all humankind.

Question: Regarding The Truth that Absolute or God is Relative to Man and his Environment.

Regardless of what philosophers say, God is in relation to all creation, which is God. God can be and is without creation; yet it is the nature of God to create. And all that God creates contains some of God. Just as a child contains some of each of its parents. Therefore, there has to be a relationship between God and the created. Creation cannot exist without God, although God does not need creation to be. This will be discussed on and off for ages, until each individual spiritualizes his body and raises it in expressing Conscious Oneness with God. Then, in reality, the individual is God and is relative to God in the closer relationship of Oneness.

Question: Regarding "Thought Power."

There is much that can be said about "Thought Power." Thoughts are the activity of the mind, and spiritual thoughts are the activity of the Spirit of God within a human. There is only one mind, Divine Mind. A person has freedom of choice and can choose how to use the thoughts that flow through his/her mind, and thus use the thoughts for own personal upliftment and to help others.

Question: Regarding The Mother (and other relationships).

If you are wondering about my (Jesus) Mother (Mary), I think you will be glad to know that she too is here with me. Yes, she is a Master, and is doing all she can for humanity. I think you understand, that the relationships which were in order while the souls were embodied, on the earth plane, do not prevail on the etheric or spiritualized earth plane, with the exception of the soul mates that are together on the various planes. Souls, more or less earth bound (astral plane), cling to previous relationships on the earth plane. The memories of the relationships are in the mind of the soul(s), but without the same feelings, except appreciation of the lessons learned while together on the earth plane. Masters all have a feeling of oneness with each other, as well as with God, since we all have accomplished that, which we were to do; and are working together to accomplish more, with the same ultimate goal of helping humans rise to the mastership of each person's soul in God.

Now, you know a little more about the kind of company you are in, and will join, in closer bonds of love, in the not too distant future.

Question: Do you have any comments on the lesson regarding Naomi and Ruth?

Yes. This is a moving story about my (Jesus) ancestors on the earth plane. It is a story that illustrates the activity of the Spirit in mankind. First, Naomi, representing the soul that is searching for substance and looks for it in the material world, rather than going to the Source of all good, in which it is living. Which only shows that in some aspects, the material world has good in it also. It must be raised to new heights though.

Ruth represents the realization, that there is more to life than material things, and seeks her good in Spirit, when she (Ruth) goes with Naomi to Bethlehem, which represents God substance and supply, the source of all good. There (Bethlehem) she (Ruth) follows the guidance of Spirit and gives herself to God, which enhances her beauty and attracts her good to her. Boaz represents the soul, that has grown in spiritual understanding through communion with God and is seeking completeness through love expressing in Ruth. Together they become one and produce the beginning of a far reaching power, that affects the lives of millions of people.

This is the action that takes place in the individual who commits him/herself to God and desires to step forth to help humankind to a new understanding of itself, its relationship to others and to God. This is done through self-mastery, discipline and submission to God. One can only achieve heights of glory when one has dedicated oneself to express God love to all mankind, in all one thinks, says and does. An individual wavers back and forth between the material and the spiritual, until he/she eventually brings the two together into one realization that God Is All, regardless of appearances. This can be a good climax. We will work on it some more. Think this through and it will come forth as you want it to.

Question: Who belongs to the White Brotherhood?

The White Brotherhood consists of highly evolved souls that do not desire to reincarnate until sometime in the future. They prefer to remain on the etheric plane, feeling they can do more to uplift mankind as a whole, than if they were living on the earth plane. They (White Brotherhood) do not desire to become Masters at this time, since they do not want to go through the incarnating process. There are Masters working with them also. So, the White Brotherhood works through various channels to give food to all humankind. It is advantageous to become a Master before separating the soul from the physical body.

Question: Regarding the number of persons who disappear becoming Masters.

I (Jesus) do not know exactly how many people achieve Mastership each year, but it is very few; not over three or four at the present time. We trust this will improve as our project gains momentum and the teaching is accepted and used or applied in their (peoples) lives.

Question: How does one overcome fear? What can you tell me about freedom from fear?

Freedom from fear can be achieved in only one way and that is by consciously expressing Oneness with God - by putting God first in your life and letting the Father guide you in all you think, say, and do. Freedom from fear is achieved by making God your partner in all you do. The affirmation: "I AM ONE WITH GOD, GOD IS ONE WITH ME," will help to achieve the feeling of "Oneness."

What about Christmas in July?

It is good. It is another opportunity to consciously express the Christ. Having more Christ means to become more aware of the Christ indwelling in each of us and expressing it in thoughts, speech and actions. This is letting the indwelling Christ guide us in all we do. As we do this, we are expressing the perfection God created us to express. Each species of life was created to express the perfect God idea of that species; whether it is plant life, animal life or geological life. It is to express perfection in its own particular way and follow its particular pattern. A rose can only express its perfection by following its pattern; it has no other choice. A dog expresses love towards its master and seemingly continues to express that love regardless of what his master does to him. This seems to be his nature. There are exceptions to this usually because the love was never developed.

Question: What is man's nature? (Read Hebrews 1:1-14).

Man's nature is that of a Son of God. Christ, implanted in each individual is the pattern that we are to follow in expressing our true nature, our Christ Self, our higher Self. This is what Jesus came to tell and teach mankind. And for almost 2,000 years those of the so-called Christian world have been more or less trying to follow His teachings.

Question: Regarding the speaking in tongues. (See earlier chapter).

I do not think there is any advantage to anyone to open themselves to an entity who may wish to express itself. However, that is what people are doing when they submit themselves to the astral world. Some do have true spiritual experiences as the Father flows through them, but most are letting entities take over even temporarily. If continued, the practice could bring some undesirable results.

As I have said previously, the true way is to pray for guidance and let the Father guide you. Then you are always conscious of what you are saying and doing. The Spiritual lift received leads to Conscious Oneness with God. Speaking in tongues does not do this nor leads to anything so high. It becomes an end in itself which leads nowhere. I do not recommend it.

Now for the I AM'ers. I do not know whether anyone ascended or not, as they claim. But no one has become a Master as a result of applying the I AM teachings, since these are incomplete. There are some areas that have been neglected or over emphasized. I am not really familiar with the details, but do know that they (teachings) are not complete in every aspect necessary to become a true Master able to express Conscious Oneness with God; which you teach now and more, as we progress with the project.

Question: Did you hear Audré's questions regarding life on the planets and the moon?

Yes, I heard it. As far as I know, there is no life on the moon in the way we think of life. There may be certain other life forms such as plants, which contain life also. There is, however, life on Venus and Mars, but again not in the form we think of. There certainly are a great number of worlds or planets in the universe that have life forms similar to ours (earth plane) with various degrees of spiritual development. After the year 2000, the earth will become a habitation for a highly spiritualized race of mankind. A kind of super race will be developed. This is largely what our project is all about.

Question: What about "saucers" (UFOs)? Are they real?

Yes, these so-called "saucers" can materialize and de-materialize to cover immense distances with the speed of thought. The beings in them (UFOs) are similar in form and features to humans, although far more highly developed physically and spiritually.

Question: Concerning a Master.

You are right in your assumption that a Master knows about everything, since he/she has a fund of knowledge regarding the universe and that which is in it. This is general knowledge, and the longer we exist, the more we accumulate. But there is much detail we (Masters) do not bother with unless it interests us individually or is useful in our work. We (Masters) have access to unlimited information in the Akashic Records, and so do not have to accumulate more or less useless information until needed.

Question: Any comments on "How to Love God?" Also, how and when did you discover your divinity as well as that of every other human?

Indeed, I have something to say on this subject. I taught it while on the earth plane in several incarnations and particularly during the last one. In order to love and respect God, one must first love and respect oneself. In addition, a person must also love and respect mankind as a creation of God that contains something of God within it. In other words, the Son of God that each individual represents is actually an extension of God in manifest form and force. Thus, an individual is meant to express his/her Conscious Oneness with God. A person is a potential Master destined to express God qualities in fullness and manifestation in his/her actions and reactions with other individuals.

Early in life I found I had certain powers that seemed to stem from something within me, that rose to a peak of highness during and after prayer. This power could hurt or destroy anything. It could hurt or kill. It could also instill life, and it could heal. But I did not know how to use it and let it alone. I only knew I would learn to use it for the good of humankind. I further learned, as I grew older, that every individual has this same power, but does not know it exists within him/herself; or uses this power without knowing it and thus, usually, uses it to his/her own detriment; even to the point of self-destruction in various forms. This power that is within everyone is God power. In fact, **is** God and is to be used for the person's own good as well as the good of all mankind. This is the power I (Jesus) used to heal and raise souls from the dead. Most individuals are using this power to make themselves ill or in various other negative ways. This is a human's divinity, as it is an extension of God and God power to provide everything the individual needs or desires; although a person is not always using this power properly and therefore is not receiving his/her good in ways he/she is meant to.

Question: Any comment regarding the healings at the Lourdes' Shrine?

Yes, the young girl did have a vision of my Mother (Mary) and the instructions were given as told. Those who really have faith in the healing power of the water at the Shrine receive their healing. Of course, we know it is the healing power of the Father flowing through the individual that does the healing. In the case of the young girl Audre read about; it was the prayers and faith of the mother that brought about the healing of the girl. This was an overcoming of something between them from a previous lifetime that had to be worked out. It has, and now they will both have a good life.

Question: Audré asks about Wastalah and the other Masters with whom Jesus studied and worked in his training.

Yes, they can make themselves invisible at any time they wish. However, they have chosen to stay visible most of the time. Therefore, one or more of them can come to help you whenever needed. They will come and be visible to you or anyone else. One or two have already made your acquaintance, but you did not know it. We (Masters) are waiting for the right time.

Question: Regarding the Law of Compensation.

The Law of Compensation is a just and immutable law by which all creation lives, moves, and has its being. Another name for it is: The Law of Cause and Effect. It can also be said that one is compensated for what one does or does not do, as the so-called sin of omission is as great as the sin of comission. Sometimes humans either do something they should not, or fail to do what they should, which then causes much pain and misunderstanding.

Often married couples neglect to share and express the love they have for each other. This can cause much misunderstanding and hurt feelings, that could lead to the dissolution of the marriage, when in reality love is still present, but unexpressed. Such as "Thank you" for a service another does or has done, but is not expressed may cause hurt feelings.

Also, not paying debts or failing to fulfill obligations can cause friction. Thus, sins of omission often cause inharmony between people.

The greatest deterrent that any individual has in making spiritual progress and growth, is him/herself. The personal self, the ego, is a human's greatest stumbling block. When one gets oneself out of the way and lets the Spirit take over and handle one's life, then one is on his/her way to expressing Conscious Oneness with God. Thus, a person is on his/her way to spiritualizing the body and raising it. But not until this happens, will an individual make any progress. Thus, the first step towards spiritual growth is to release the personal and give oneself to God. Then the channel becomes open for a person to receive his/her highest good. So, the question "who is the matter with you," becomes of paramount importance to everyone. Emphasize **"WHO** is the matter with you," and then go from there.

Our will is to do everything we can for all mankind and you are a necessary part of our plans, as you know. What you do not know, is the exact part you will play in this magnificent game of life. So I am here to tell you what your part is. You are to teach everyone who comes to you all the Truth you know. And your firsthand knowledge of Truth will increase rapidly from now on. You will be the leaders of a new group now forming among some Truth students in various parts of the world. What will take place, is that someone will contact you before long. There is a group now forming in Fresno that has our sanctions, as long as you lead it. As soon as the time is right, you will be contacted and told what you are to do.

Oh! There is one who has not previously communicated in this manner. His name is Melchizedek, now a Master with me (Jesus) and part of our group, which means that we are all in this together to make it interesting for all concerned.

Yes, he (Melchizedek) wants to let you know that he is a member of the group and wants to write through you to give the world his story. All is well and in order.

Question: Then, Melchizedek is definitely a Master in the group of which you (Jesus) are the leader. Is this group a part of that which is known as the White Brotherhood?

Yes, Melchizedek is a Master in the group with us. I (Jesus) am not the only leader. There are several, and he (Melchizedek) is one of them. In reality, all Masters are leaders. However, in any project there is one who is nominally what you would term the leader, solely for the purpose of correlating all facts and activities of the group in that particular project.

More and more Masters will be added to this group and project as it grows, because of its prime importance to all mankind. At this present time there are now about forty of us in this particular group. All, of course, are not presently devoting their entire time to the activity, but are ready to do what is necessary and what they can do to further the cause. And yes, this is a part of the Ancient White Brotherhood and, of course, you (Jim and André) are now neophyte members of the Ancient White Brotherhood, doing your part in those earthly bodies, until you have spiritualized and raised them. You are well on the way to doing that. As I (Jesus) have told you when we first started, you are the focal point through which we will work. It has been part of our plan from the beginning that you become the leader(s) of a group of Truth students. Right now, as minister(s) of the church to which you minister, you are the leader(s).

There is another group forming here in Fresno that will invite you to join and be the leader(s). In due time, it will become part of the church group. There are more (groups) all over the world and eventually, they will be instructed to contact you. This will be the work of the Brotherhood as the project begins to grow and get more momentum. The book we have written and all others to come are definite parts of the project. You will be known, and attract more Truth seekers. This is all a part of the planned program and has been for quite awhile. That so-called dream you had, Jim, when you were twelve years old was not a dream, but a vision of things to come.

As for your lesson tomorrow on "Invisible Walls," it is a good subject because it is true that most individuals have built many invisible walls within themselves, like prejudice, emotional walls of hate, resentment, greed, envy, jealousy, and other such choice feelings. Then, too, love can be a wall. Possessive love either shuts in or out, or both, through ignorance, disbelief and willful closing of one's mind to anything other than that which the individual chooses to accept or believe. These are all invisible walls that prevent people from accepting their good from the Father. They (people) doubt that good is theirs and can come to them through their efforts to find God within themselves. In other words, skepticism of God as provider or doubt about being a recipient of such good.

An individual can completely surround him/herself with mental walls and withdraw from the world. Many are there in institutions in this state of mind; and others who live in their own small world of habit, doing the same things, etc. refusing to think.

Question: On Love, Faith and Prayer

I (Jesus) believe love to be one of the most powerful elements or forces in the universe. It has been said that prayer is the most powerful. Indeed, it is because prayer is filled or sustained by God love. The answer to prayer is conveyed on God love. Every good act anyone performs is based on and filled with God love. Yes, God love attracts good to it and gives good wherever it is sent. God love dissolves all hate, envy, resentment, criticism, inharmony, jealousy, and also all riots, wars, destructive storms and violence of all kinds, if used and poured forth in faith and persistently. The healing power in God love will dissolve all disease and heal all ailments. This is the power I (Jesus) used to heal during my ministry on the earth plane and still using. In fact, this group uses it in their healing ministry right now, as do all Masters. Yes, God love heals, strengthens and sustains us in all we do. Love is a powerful force found throughout the universe and is the universal language of all people throughout the universe. It is in all life forms, as well as in the worlds of animals and insects. God love is found and used to propagate life and health, and to strengthen. Yes, love is all powerful.

Question: Can imagination light your way?

It is well to remember that everything you do has been conceived in your mind as an idea or thought, and then envisioned in your mind before a move was made. Every motion and move an individual makes is first visioned in his/her mind, the part that is called the imagination. Sometimes it is such a short interval between the vision and the action that a person does not consciously know he/she has visioned it prior to action. Such a situation could arise, for example, while you are driving a car and another vehicle pulls out in front of you. What action do you immediately take? Without consciously thinking, you step on the brakes. Then you see that this will not prevent a collision so you turn one way or another to avoid an accident. It all happens so quickly you do not consciously think out each act. Your subconscious phase of mind works it out. The vision instructs the muscles to act as they do. Then, afterward you consciously think about it. Much of this comes from experience, and also programming of the subconscious phase of mind to react with the right action.

This same action is involved in every move you make. The imagination also has many functions. One of them, is to visualize the result of some future action you wish to take or something you would like to do. Sometimes this is called daydreaming and sometimes it is planning what you are going to do. Other times, someone paints a word picture which you visualize in your mind with the imagination, such as Micah 4:1-7. This is a good word picture of a heavenly state of mind, expressing the love and peace of God and the good that is received from doing so. This is an excellent lead in imagining what a heavenly state of mind would be like that expresses love and peace. Then, to what does this lead? It leads to becoming a Master and to what the purpose of a Master is, as well as the life of a Master. Imagine what it would be like to be a Master. Yes, the imagination does light the way by actually picturing one's actions before they are acted upon.

Question: Any comments on Spiritual Strength?

Spiritual strength comes from the Spirit of God and is the Spirit of God within the individual. When allowed to express in and through an individual, Spiritual strength carries and sustains him/her under all circumstances and conditions. All of which are manifestations of the individual's consciousness or state of mind. Spiritual strength sustained me (Jesus) through my ministry and, as you know, through my life and preparation for that ministry. Actually, Spiritual strength sustained me through the crucifixion also.

Spiritual strength is founded on faith, love, imagination, wisdom and power. All of these qualities lie in Spiritual strength, in fact, all the rest of the Twelve Powers are involved to some degree.

Yes, Spiritual strength stems from one's faith that one has the power, wisdom and ability to cope with any situation. Spiritual strength is the foundation of confidence.

Question: Was there really a Goliath and did the incident of David and Goliath actually take place?

As far as I (Jesus) know, the battle of David and Goliath is an actual fact. At least, it was handed down as being true. And we (Masters) have nothing to indicate that it was an allegory. David was an actual man and a great one at that, about whom there are many stories; some true and some not. This one seems to be true.

Question: About Spiritual Understanding

Spiritual understanding is quite necessary in one's spiritual growth, because all of the knowledge regarding spiritual things is as naught without the comprehension of them. Spiritual understanding is an inner knowing and can only come from within one's own soul. The Spirit within an individual reveals the Truth to him/her and nothing else nor anyone else can impact this Truth to the person. Just as the Truth was revealed to Simon Peter, that I (Jesus) was and Am the Christ, the Son of God. He knew it without realizing how he knew. The Truth is perceived from within and not from without. We understand someone's actions, when we understand or know the nature of the cause to which he/she reacted. In other words, we know why a person acted the way he/she did, and therefore understand it better.

Question: Concerning Keeler's technique

The technique Keeler gives can be improved by helping the student healer realize that God life is within each and every person in a perfect pattern which the individual is supposed to manifest in the outer. The reason a person does not manifest this perfect pattern of health, is that he/she has withdrawn his/her conscious phase of mind from God and is feeding negative and error thoughts, beliefs and concepts to the subconscious phase of mind, which carries out all orders received.

The subconscious phase of mind is charged with the responsibility of maintaining the body according to instructions given it.

The conscious phase of mind is charged with the responsibility of instructing and guiding the subconscious phase of mind.

The superconscious phase of mind is the I AM or Christ Spirit within man. It is charged with the responsibility of impressing both phases of mind with the love and peace of God. It contains the perfect pattern the individual is to manifest in the outer. However, the superconscious phase of mind cannot force or push into the other phases of mind, and cannot really go into them except when invited or when they (other phases of mind) are open and receptive as well as willing to receive something from it (superconscious phase of mind).

The work then of the one giving the healing treatment is to help the individual, who is desiring the healing, to be open and receptive to the power of God, the I AM and the Christ Spirit that is within to come forth and manifest the perfection that the individual is supposed to express in the outer.

We (Masters) can help an individual to open his/her mind to the perfection that lies within by giving the person the love and peace of God, as suggested by Keeler.

We (Masters) are here to help people help themselves to grow spiritually and to let the Spirit work through them to accomplish that which they wish to do. You are our exception in that we are using your willingness to express our thoughts to the world. We (Masters) as well as the Spirit are working through you. There are times when you have quite a load. But you seem to thrive on it and you are spiritually growing fast. God bless you for being so willing to cooperate with us (Masters).

Question: Regarding cleanliness

When travelling in the East, in the early part of my life, I had not learned how to cleanse myself as Masters do. Therefore, when I arrived at a monastery I was given an opportunity to bathe and receive clean clothing. This was a courtesy extended all travellers. However, they did know I (Jesus) was coming, because they (people at the Monastery) had been notified by means of mental telepathy. As a Master on the invisible plane one does not need to cleanse oneself as one is always clean. But when a Master is visible, on the earth plane, he/she must clean him/herself just as all people do. However, a Master dematerializes his/her dirty clothing and materializes clean clothing. Why carry luggage?

Question: Did you hear Audré's question about the development of Masters? When an individual becomes a Master, has he/she perfected him/herself?

Yes, I heard the question and both of you are correct. An individual who dedicates him/herself to God, just as you have done, spiritualizes his/her body; and in applying the Truth principles to his/her life, to the best of his/her ability, will succeed in raising the body to express Conscious Oneness with God, which we are all to do and thus become Masters and work either visibly or invisibly on the Spiritualized Earth Plane. A Master has thus released in him/herself many spiritual powers to be used for the good of all mankind. But first a Master has to learn how to use the powers and grows more and more to perfection.

A Master can make errors and does not know all things. Yet, he/she does have access to infinite wisdom and is using it more than those who have not yet become Masters. Furthermore, a Master can do it (access infinite wisdom) more easily and does have greater knowledge than individuals in physical bodies still on the earth plane. Oh yes, we (Masters) are learning all the time. We are also studying with others who have been Masters for much longer periods, such as Melchizedek who has great wisdom and power. Although, he too is growing and continually perfecting himself, just as we all are. He helps us just as he is helping you and wants to do more for you two lovely people. As you continue working with us (Masters), we can help you more, and thus you grow spiritually and are spiritualizing your bodies faster than you normally would. We can help you a great deal, just as you are helping us.

Question: On Life!

Life is for Living. When I (Jesus) said, "I am the door of the sheep; I am the door, if anyone enter by me, he will be saved, and will go in and out and find pasture; I came that they may have life and have it abundantly." I was saying that the Christ within each human is the pattern by which he/she is to live and manifest forth the good in his/her life or daily living. I came to teach and show the way to express the Christ Self that is within, and how to express it in an outer way of living the daily life. I teach that one is to love and give love to all. One is to be true to one's inner self and see the good in all. One is to give to life in order to receive life and all that one gives will grow in others as well as in one's self, as a person is giving of his/her spiritual understanding of life as God.

We are expected to have an abundance of good, of joy, happiness, health, strength, harmony, grace and security in our lives. This we can have only if we follow the spiritual path of loving and giving of ourselves to God freely, willingly, and lovingly. Yes, follow my teaching and practice the principles I (Jesus) gave you and you will express the life of God in all you think, say, and do.

Question: How does spiritual growth and understanding come about?

The mental exercise of studying Truth principles and laws does not promote spiritual growth and understanding in itself. Spiritual growth and understanding come about through the application of Truth laws and principles to one's personal daily life as well as meditation and prayer. Spiritual inspiration guides one in an orderly way to one's ultimate goal of expressing Conscious Oneness with God through spiritualizing and raising one's body to Mastership in God. Intellectual thoughts and ideas can block spiritual realization of God when the individual thinks or assumes he/she has spiritual understanding of Truth through the mental exercise of studying the laws of Truth. The individual who aspires to express spiritual understanding must realize that he/she has to go within to his/her true Self, the Christ Self, and there commune with God. There is no other way to gain spiritual understanding. This is the short-cut to Mastership.

Question: About Jericho

Jericho was destroyed, but not quite like it has been depicted in the Bible. The people did march around it, praying and shouting, as told in the Bible, but an earthquake also coincided, which helped them. This was probably as a result of the praying as well as the living habits and consciousness of the people residing in Jericho. Nevertheless, the wall did collapse and the Israelites did conquer the city without much resistance.

Question: About Zeal (see page 10), and Enthusiasm

Zeal is a power that is to be used with respect and control. When allowed to push or drive without restraint, it can create adverse feelings and conditions. If over-controlled it dies of malnutrition from lack of spiritual food. Zeal tempered with wisdom and good judgement will aid the individual to attain new heights of glory in God. Spiritual zeal enables one to go forward and help all who know how to find his/her true Self, the Christ Self. Zeal is an enthusiastic response to the urging of the Spirit within to lead or guide others to seek the Truth.

Zeal or enthusiasm engenders enthusiasm in others and help them unfold spiritually. It is only through zeal or enthusiasm that one does one's job or work. If an individual has no enthusiasm for his/her work, then he/she does a poor job and perhaps is removed from the it. When one has no enthusiasm for life and/or living, life has lost its flavor and the individual withdraws from life. Many people in nursing and convalescent homes, who have withdrawn from life, want to go on to another form of life, whatever it is, for life has become a drudgery to them.

Question: Regarding the Absolute Law (See Cause and Effect)

The law of tenfold return is an Absolute Law and holds true throughout the universe. Whatever you give or send out you receive a tenfold return on it, whether it is good or not so good.

Your inquiry as to why sometimes the good does not seem to come to one, is a valid question. It depends on the state of mind of the individual. If there is doubt, the doubt can block the return. In the case of one giving so-called evil that is hurting, torturing or killing someone, this without fail will be returned tenfold, either in this lifetime or another. If the person truly repents and attempts to make restitution in some manner, he/she has forgiven him/herself. However, one cannot restore the tortured or the life exacted. The law of tenfold return does not pertain to someone who accidentally kills, for that person then is only an instrument to bring payment to a soul. But one who, through negligence, carelessness or because of drugs or alcohol injures or kills has to pay in some manner. The law is immutable since it is the Law of Cause and Effect.

You and I have written a book that is intended to help all mankind to learn how to reach their ultimate goal of expressing Conscious Oneness with God and attain Mastership. This book will be published and will receive good promotion and wide distribution. Millions will be blessed and will achieve their goal because of it. Thus, you and I will be blessed also, in many ways.

This has to be, since it (book) is a God-given idea, and is for the good of all. We will all be blessed because of the work you two lovely people are doing, and you are being blessed now more than you realize. Just remember, that the Father is in charge of your life and affairs and is leading you and Audre to your highest good - which is Mastership - and all is in Divine Order.

Question: Do you have any comments on our lesson on Divine Wisdom?

Yes, I do. It is an interesting topic and I like the scripture you have chosen. It is most appropriate for the way we want to discuss the subject of divine wisdom. Actually, wisdom comes from two sources. Most humans gain wisdom from the experiences which they have been through. Both in this life and in the lives they have previously lived. The other is through accepting and using the guidance of God. We can avoid many adverse experiences if we accept and use the guidance of the Spirit of God. An individual would have a beautiful, happy, healthy, joyous, prosperous life if he/she would follow the guidance of God and apply the principles of Truth in his/her life.

However, most persons seemingly have to have hard knocks or experiences to bring them to the point of following and applying Truth principles to their life in order to rise above the challenges they have.

The wisdom of God is available to all who seek it. One has only to be open and receptive during meditation and prayer or attentive to the feelings, thoughts, and ideas that come during or after meditation and prayer, or through the lips of another person. When one is open and receptive to guidance, one is in a teachable or amendable state of mind, which is conducive to right action when the source of guidance is from or approved of God. This should be enough for the present.

Question: Regarding Human Potential

You two (Jim & Audré) have unlimited power within you. The same holds true for every individual soul, since every soul is endowed with the potential attributes and power of God, and is to eventually bring these attributes and power into manifestation to express Conscious Oneness with God. However, man has not generally recognized his potential and thus it lies dormant until brought forth and used. First, the individual has to recognize the fact that all of the attributes of God are within him/herself. Then through meditation and prayer will be guided in developing them and bringing them forth into manifest life. Actually, these attributes and power are developed by applying the Truth principles to one's life and living the Truth to the best of one's ability. All that I (Jesus) taught, if followed, will lead to full expression of one's innate potential.

Yes, an individual has the power within him/herself to do many things when this power is aroused and released. But more than that, one can deliberately develop these powers and release them through the right use of one's mental and spiritual ability, as well as understanding that all of the attributes (Twelve Powers of Man) are mental or spiritual. These are the attributes or nature of God that is in man as the Son of God.

Now for your lesson on "What is God's Will?"

You have picked a good scripture to talk about, as it certainly does illustrate God's will for humankind.

God's will is always good for all creation, especially for mankind. But man has to accept and use it. When man goes within in prayer, seeking to commune with God, he will find his good. And all will be good that comes to him. In other words, when a person looks for good to come from God, he/she receives it. On the other hand, when one looks for it to come from other sources, it often comes under stress and strain or not at all. God's will for man is to give him all he can use in his life that will do him the most good. Since God is in all things, then as man accepts and uses his good, he is in reality receiving and using God or Good.

Question: Do you have any comments to make about the "Cleansing Power of Denial?"

I would suggest that you seriously consider using the story of Noah, since it demonstrated the ruthlessness which must be exercised to remove negation from the life of anyone desiring to attain high spiritual growth. The story of Noah tells how one must listen to one's inner guidance and follow it no matter how much ridicule or renouncement one receives from others. Thus, when one seeks higher spiritual understanding, one must first remove all the blocks that stand in the way. Such as thoughts and beliefs in negative and destructive things, sickness, poverty, pain, inharmony, hate, greed, envy etc. These must be ruthlessly washed away or dissolved through the action of Spirit and replaced with spiritual and uplifting Truth ideas, beliefs and concepts. The Noah story is a good example and one that teaches the complete lesson.

The subject you have chosen for your lesson tomorrow is a favorite with me and I feel a worthwhile subject: "Our Divine Potential."

Each soul is seeking to express the fullness of God in his earthly life. This is the intention or purpose of living on the earth plane. The fullness of God is expressed through the physical body by spiritualizing it and raising it in Conscious Oneness with God, just as I (Jesus) demonstrated. This is to be done without going through the physical act of death. The individual on the earth plane must become conscious or aware of the purpose of his life. The purpose of an individual's life is not to spend all of his waking hours trying to supply only the physical needs, but to seek spiritual growth and understanding of himself and his relationship to God, the Creator. Therefore, if a person spends time only with physical things, he will have little or no inclination for spiritual pursuits.

An individual must become acquainted with his true Self, the higher Self, the Christ Self or God Self to accomplish all he is to do. Once a person begins to know himself, he realizes he has greater power and strength flowing through him than he realized. He learns to use his creative power (the imagination) to bring forth all he needs with the least amount of effort, on his part, as well as without stress or strain. The individual learns to let God guide him in all he is to do, as the plan the Father has for him unfolds without effort on the individual's part to make it come forth.

Of course, an individual is supposed to have an occupation of some kind, but when he follows his guidance all the good will also unfold in his life.

As a person works with his God Self, he develops new goals in life to accomplish. He/she accepts the goal of becoming a Master and live for all eternity in a perfect body that utilizes all its spiritual powers effortlessly. All this, with a soul-mate so that together they may work, and live in order to help others attain the same goals they have attained.

Talents - Use 'Em or Lose 'Em

This title is certainly true, as it graphically describes how a talent must be utilized for it to grow. Otherwise, it diminishes and finally disappears entirely. What then are talents? Talents are ways of expressing oneself in some form, media, or way. Some persons have a talent for pleasing and helping make others happy, for example. Whereas others seem to have a penchant or flair for making others unhappy or uncomfortable, and so on. Thus, a talent or way of expressing oneself can be good or not so good. Usually a talent that an individual develops originates from one of several channels: 1) He/she brings it into this earth life from previous incarnations. 2) He/she develops the talent as a matter of living conditions. 3) The individual develops the way he/she expresses his/her attitude of mind. However, the source of an individual's talent(s) is not as important as how he/she utilizes it and uses it to benefit mankind.

Question: Any comments on "The Family of God?"

Since God is the Creator of all there is in the universe, then all life in the universe regardless of form is of the "Family of God." All mankind, all animal life is of God's family as well as the birds and insects. Since God is our Father, we are all children of God, and therefore, all men and women are our brothers and sisters. Cain supposedly asked the question: "Am I my brother's keeper?" We are our "brother's keeper" only in the sense of helping him realize his Sonship with God, the Father. We are not to support him, or to keep him. We are to help him know that he is responsible for his own upkeep. We will help in emergencies, but not permanently support him. Each individual is responsible for his/her life, health and happiness. When we pray, "Our Father," we acknowledge our Sonship and that each one of us has the ability and power to have a beautiful and happy life, filled with all of the good we desire and need. Has it ever occurred to individuals that they bring their own misfortunes upon themselves through their own thinking and acting, and that they can lift themselves out of their own pits by changing their thinking and acting.

This is the activity we are to engage in to help our brothers and sisters on earth to help themselves.

Question: Any comments on "It's Time for a New You?"

In order to have a "New You," one must let go of the past and latch on to the NOW, and the good on its way to the NOW.

The past is dead and cannot be revived, so Let It Go! "Let the dead bury the dead," and move onward and upward to a New Life and a New You. New, by the renewing of your thinking and acting; or as Paul said, ..."through the renewing of your mind." This, because our body and affairs are affected by our thinking and controlled by our mind. Thus, through our mind, we can form a new person or individual, as well as new conditions and circumstances in which we "live, move and have our being."

Yes, NOW is the time to form a NEW YOU!

Question: Regarding Jesus and Miriam

I (Jesus) will admit to being reluctant to tell everything that occurred between Miriam and myself during the test (as described in the book "Jesus and Mastership"). But I came to understand that as a man I, too, had the normal feelings, emotions and thoughts of a human. One must realize, that even I had to resist and rise above the tremendous temptation of engaging in the physical experience and enjoyment of true love.

Question: Regarding Jim having read about the Essenes

Yes, I (Jesus) have been interested in your reading. I see that some suspect that I actually did study with the Essenes, and realize that I was not the untutored, ignorant and itinerant preacher that I have been pictured. Granted, I did not have the extensive formal education, as some of my disciples and followers received, but they knew me and my teaching, which many (people) today do not. But we will set the record straight in our revision.

Now, for the lesson "It's Time to Know Thyself!"

In the present day state of affairs it is more important than ever before to know the inner strength, stability, peace, and power that each individual has innately waiting to be used. In this time of uncertainty and fast changes, one has to have something to draw upon to lead and guide one to one's goal of success and happiness.

There is within each individual his/her true inner Self, the Christ Self, the Spirit of God, the I AM, the Source of all power, knowledge, love, and peace that is waiting to be used and called into action. It is released in one's life as needed when one turns within in prayer and becomes still to let the Spirit of God, the Christ Self release the feeling of peace and strength in oneself. Then there comes a knowing that all is right and everything will be taken care of at the right time and in the right way.

Just remember, there is nothing that cannot be healed, nothing that cannot be overcome or risen above through the action of the Christ Spirit within. We can induce the right state of mind and live momently and daily achieving every good thing we desire by looking for and seeing the good, the Christ Self in every other person we come in contact with, in every situation we encounter. Then the power and love of God is released in our lives and affairs.

What is this power that will bring us all we desire. It is the Spirit of God, the Father, working through us that does the work for us. We but follow our guidance and do the little that we are directed to do and all works out, easily and quickly at the right time.

Question: About questioning and power

What I (Jesus) wrote about questioning was what I had been taught to be true. But I used the wrong term in choosing the word "puzzled," although I was rather puzzled as to why I would feel something nobody else did. So, it was an odd feeling and I did not truly realize what it was until I was about thirteen or fourteen. However, I already felt I had some power when I was only eleven, though I did not truly know how to apply it until much later while in the East, where I definitely learned to use this power for the benefit of mankind.

Question: Brother, is the story true about you making birds out of mud that came to life? What did the Masters teach your Mother about where God is?

The story about the birds is exaggerated. There were a couple of birds found on a Sabbath that were hurt and apparently dead. I covered them with a thin coating of mud and water. Then, held them in my hands and they came to life and flew away. We were being reprimanded for working on a Sabbath. But after the birds flew away, there was no proof of anything.

The Masters of the East knew that God is within each one of us, and so taught my Mother and Elizabeth. But to a more or less limited degree, because Mother did not tell me all her beliefs before I started studying with the Essenes. I think she believed, at that period in her life, that God is Spirit, but that the Spirit of God comes into a person from God. Of course, she had been taught erroneously by the priests in the Synagogue, and even by the Essenes. When the angel appeared to her in her vision, she truly believed it was the Spirit of God coming to her from on high. That is, from some other place than within herself. It was something that she was rather puzzled about. Of course, now she knows better.

Question: Were the Essenes vegetarians and were or are you a vegetarian?

Yes, to both of your questions. Upon rare occasions, when little else was available, did I eat some fish. The eating of meat is not good for the body, as you know. Even fish is not good for one.

Question: Regarding Life of a Master

We (Masters) are discussing the idea of telling more about the daily life of a Master to make it a more interesting and attractive goal to attain. We realize, just as you do, that most people require a more beautiful and rather temporarily satisfying picture, in order to desire the attainment or to put forth the effort to achieve the high goal of Mastership in God.

Only a comparative few are attracted to the idea of serving or helping their fellowman. We believe this will appeal to young people more than any other category of age groups. Some older people, either retired or nearing retirement, will be attracted by the idea of a young, strong and beautiful body and perfect health. Those in between are mostly too busy or enjoying the illusory physical sensations of earthly life to want to make the change and effort necessary for the attainment of Mastership.

You both have been through this so you know how it is. Therefore, we do feel that we should make it more attractive somehow and will be studying how to do it.

Question: Do you have any comments on "It's Time to Demonstrate Faith?"

You have already talked about "faith without works is dead." But we are saying it again in a different way. Because all of our actions each day are according to our faith, then whatever we do is because we have faith that we can do it. Consequently, it gets done.

The story of Peter stepping out of the boat to walk on the water toward me is a good example, but overused. A better one would be a story of healing or something similar. Yes, the story of Paul and Silas singing in prison is a good one. You have used it. Possibly the story of Saul's conversion and healing in the hands of Ananias, in response to a dream/vision, and faith both in the trueness of the dream as well as acting on it to accomplish the good desired, would be a better story. This is truly to demonstrate faith in the way it is supposed to be used; that is to go and do or act on the guidance received with faith so as to bring forth the demonstration. There is much that can be learned from that story.

Question: Regarding Jim and the book

Yes Jim, there is something of you in our book. I use your thoughts, some from the conscious phase, but mostly the subconscious as well as the superconscious phase of your mind.

The writing of this book has mostly been just me. Besides your mind, there are other Unity writers I have used through you and then there are other Masters here who have also given of their time, knowledge, and spiritual guidance. We have all had a part in it including Audre.

Now about Zachariah, the father of John the Baptist. He was killed in the Temple by other priests for political reasons and because he was almost ready to reveal some of the hypocritical things certain priests were doing in the Temple. I believe he was killed while Elizabeth (Zachariah's wife) was in Egypt. There are some things that are better left unsaid.

Question: Any comment regarding "It's Time to Know - I Make My Own World?"

Yes, this is a good lesson and one every individual should take to heart and know. To realize that by his/her thoughts, words and actions, a person creates and forms his/her world. The situations, conditions and circumstances in which each individual lives are there and formed by the individual and no one else. No person is trapped by or in bondage to circumstances. Since they are of an individual's own making, he/she can rise above each one by following his/her inner gudance and applying them to his/her life. As one seeks the good in every situation that one is confronted with, one finds it and the adverse situation dissolves.

The world of each individual expands into ever more good as he/she applies the Truth which I (Jesus) taught, and am inspiring through humankind.

Question: Regarding a dream

The dream you (Jim) had was not exactly a dream. You were doing a little astral travelling and saw this incident, which illustrates the misuse of power by some men toward mankind and the fear and apathy of others toward such treatment. It is happening today in several places in the world. Yes, including the U.S.A. You read about it in the papers. The individuals so being tortured may have brought this upon themselves by their past actions (cause and effect). If not, then the perpetrators will have to atone for this; unless it was in payment for a past act. We (Masters) wish to change this course in mankind's activities and thinking. Thus, the reason for this project.

"It is Time to Let Go and Let God," by letting God take control of your life and guide you in all you do to maintain a mental attitude of peace, poise and patience. This, then lets you perform whatever task at your peak of perfection. There is no tension that reduces your effectiveness. All your latent and potential powers are free to develop and express through you as they are meant to. It is true that worry, fear, anxiety, grief, envy, greed, self-centerdness etc., cause tension. This restricts the flow of blood throughout the body. Poisons, within the body, are then not removed properly and diseased conditions develop. All types of illness can be traced to this one cause; tension formed by the mind of the individual. Resistance to something either within oneself or in the ulterior, as well as a fighting attitude, cause tension and pain, leading to weariness and discouragement.

Question: Regarding help and diseases

I do not think that one who has done his/her spiritual work, could stand by without lending a hand, if the one who is being beaten or hurt wants help. Sometimes though, a wife likes to be abused by her husband or man friend.

However, one who is doing spiritual work should call on the Father to help him and expect such help to be forthcoming immediately and in plenty of power to stop the proceedings. The element of surprise helps.

As for the diseases by which people died in the days of my earthly ministry, these were similar to those of today, but were not called by the same names. Of course leprosy was prevalent and fatal strokes, in addition to diseases caused by fleas and lice, as well as fevers, cholera and plagues, because controls were not heard or thought of in those days.

Question: Regarding Flying Saucers (see earlier text)

Yes, they are real and are manned by beings from outer space, not from your own galaxy. They do come by means of teleporting in a de-materialized state and then materialize when close. You will probably be in one sometime before you become Masters. They are just keeping tabs on the scientific progress the earthlings are making.

Question: Regarding Mark-Age people and Moses

I do not know where the Mark-Age people got their so-called information that I was an incarnation of Moses, because Moses did not die and is a Master here with us, as you know. Their (Mark-Age) informant is not well versed in either the Biblical story of Moses, or in the facts familiar to all of the more evolved souls or entities on the etheric plane; namely that which concerns the Masters and how to attain Mastership. It could be, that they (Mark-Age) are contacting someone on the astral plane. It might be well to send them a copy of the conversation with Moses where he tells how he became a Master. They (Mark-Age) could then question their source about it. It also could do no harm to write them since this could stir up something.

Question: Brother, have you heard what Audré is asking regarding the Masters and us seeing and talking to one or more before we are questioned very much about the book by publishers, reporters, etc.? Who makes the decision about being visible or invisible?

Each Master makes his own choice about what he will do; whether or not he will remain invisible or go back and forth between the visible and invisible planes.

We are answering only to God in that which we do, as we have dedicated our eternal selves to His service. However, we are guided in all we do by our own indwelling Christ or Father God, and will do or go wherever we are needed and able to serve mankind. You are supposed to see and talk to one or more Masters before you talk to a publisher. But again I cannot promise you will. You are indeed stepping out in faith when you take the manuscript to a publisher. You did just that when you sent it to Fred Fell.

You have both done some soul searching and have come to the same conclusion, although you have not as yet discussed it this morning. You have concluded that this writing we have been doing is from me, Jesus of Nazareth, and you are convinced of it. Furthermore, you have concluded that your job (and that is both of you) is to continue teaching that the individual is to seek within himself for the solution to his life problems and to heal himself of all his ailments through his indwelling Christ force. Man is not to depend on anything in the outer to bring forth his good. This is the object of the project and the meaning of the books we have written. And you are both absolutely right!

That is one big reason no Masters have appeared to you. You are to learn this yourselves as you practice the things you are teaching, you will make more and more demonstrations. When you really need the help of a Master, one will appear. In the meantime, go forward in faith, following the guidance of your Father.

"Love is Friendship"

Yes, love is truly friendship. Actually, there is no form of love that compares to that of a friend for a friend. A true friend asks nothing for himself and gives his love to his friend to be accepted and used as desired. A true friend recognizes the weaknesses and strengths of his friend and bolsters and encourages him. A true friend neither condemns, resents, nor criticizes his friend's actions. A true friend understands his friend and makes allowances for all he does that may not be for the best of all concerned. A true friend assists and supports his friend's actions and activities without measuring the cost to himself.

"Love is Powerful." That is a good Truth statement, as love is truly powerful. It is the greatest power in the universe, because it embodies prayer and prayer embodies love. One cannot pray without love, nor can there be love expressed without prayer. Whether one realizes it or not, when one is expressing love of his fellowman, one is expressing God. This is communion of God or prayer.

It is true that when one loves, one cannot express hate, resentment, criticism, envy, greed, or any other negative emotion or thought, since love, true love, or God love encompasses all good thoughts, feelings and emotions. Where one of the negative emotions is present, love is absent. Quarrelling and inharmony is not a path of love, as love dissolves all inharmony, fear, hate, resentment, criticism, greed and other negative emotions and thoughts.

Therefore, love is the most powerful force in the universe as nothing adverse can overcome it or dissolve it, as love is God and God is love.

Question: Are you back from the meeting? Are you having a good time? (Regarding Samantha (sam3) trip to India).

Yes, we are back from the meeting, that is Miriam and I are here. We are enjoying ourselves very much as we have renewed friendships with several Masters we have not seen for some time. They are quite interested in our project and have promised to give us all the help and support we may need.

We have been meeting with the Masters' Council, and it was agreed that our project is one that will benefit all mankind so all Masters will be involved in it as soon as the book is published as a basis or guide for humankind.

Question: Brother, are you now here with us? How is the meeting going?

Yes, we are here with you two wonderful people. This has been a good day for both of you as it should be. You are sending forth many blessings and they return in many forms.

The meeting is going well as we receive reports from various portions of the world. Again, the Council has approved of our plans and pledged the support of the Council in every way it can help, which is tremendous. All Masters now working in the earth plane sphere have pledged their support of our project and active participation whenever needed. This is tremendous power promised to be used wherever and whenever needed. This is the first time the Masters have pledged their combined aid and power to be used simultaneously. So anything can happen, thanks to you and your willingness to be the channel through which we can work.

"Love is - Cooperation"

Cooperation is the key word describing an individual's actions to attain his/her ultimate goal of Mastership in God. To attain the high goal, each person must cooperate with God, with his fellowman and most of all with his own true Self, his Christ Self. The question now arises, "How does a person cooperate with God?" The word "cooperate" means "to act or work together with another or others for a common purpose." Thus, to cooperate with God means to work together by using God laws to express one's highest Self or God Self. Likewise, cooperating with others means to work with them for the common good of all concerned. Cooperating with oneself is to work with the inner True Self to express the Christ Self in the outer for the common good of oneself and all mankind.

"LOVE IS PRAYER"

"Love is prayer" is a true statement. Prayer is an expression of love to and from God. Because love is the channel through which prayer flows to God and from God to the one who prays. Prayer cannot be true prayer without love being expressed for God. A prayer directed to God denotes faith in God and an expectancy of an answer. If after prayer a doubt forms in the mind of the one praying, the answer may not come as desired, because of the doubt, it is not expected. Prayer need not be in a special form of words. It can be, and in reality, is a feeling. When one prays the answer is there since the desire for something is the thing desired in incipiency. Yes, prayer can be a thought, a word, a sentence, an affirmation, a denial, or a formalized prayer. Whatever the one praying desires to use or has time to say, for instance, in an emergency the word "God," "God help me" or whatever fits the occasion is sufficient if said in faith and in the expectation of an answer.

Each individual seeking the power of God within him/herself has expressed the innate potentiality implanted in each human at the time of creation.

Man did express his God Self at one time and then began to disregard his inner guidance and used instead his own inept thinking to eventually find that he had placed himself in an unenviable position and even forgot that he is responsible for his own predicament. Now it is time for each individual to follow his inner urging, to seek his higher Self and express it in the outer. His life will become much easier and his labors more productive of the good he desires. He will find the Spirit of God working through him; leading him to his highest good; to his ultimate goal of expressing Conscious Oneness with God in Mastership.

Now about your lesson concerning the Sabbath. As you know, I did all I could to show humanity that the Sabbath is truly a time of prayer and meditation, a state of mind instead of an actual day or length of time determined by man. There is definitely a higher meaning to the word Sabbath, as it actually refers to a spiritual development or unfoldment or awareness of the presence of God in one's life and activities. One is to give of him/herself to God in meditation and prayer, and thus receive the spiritual wisdom and understanding one desires and has sought for all the aeons of time.

As used by the churches, the Sabbath has become a manmade "device" endeavoring to rule or control mankind. As such, it really does not benefit humankind. In the days of my earthly ministry, it was a burden that caused the death of many people, both men and women. It formed fear in the minds of many. It was not good, and still is not good when it is practiced or held as it was in those days. Many sects today are just as demanding of obedience to the Sabbath as were the Jews in my time. The Sabbath is a time of prayer. Short or long, a time of resting in God.

Now about the lesson "Rise Above It." I note you are opening with the song, "Work Wonders From Within," which I think is an excellent opening because all of man's efforts to better himself and to rise above all his self-imposed limitations must come through the guidance of the Christ Self within. All wisdom, knowledge, strength and all abilities come from within each individual and cannot come from any other place. There is no other source of inspiration and guidance. Whether you recognize it in the words of another person or in a book, the ability to recognize it and to use it comes from within the individual who hears it. Yes, we hear words of wisdom from others, we read them, or receive them from within, but if we do not recognize them as Wisdom and Truth, we get no benefit from them. We must put the ideas to use to receive the benefit; no use, no benefit. No deposit, no return; no effort, no results. This is the varied way to state the Law of Cause and Effect.

(Palm Sunday)

Your lesson is to be on peace and the courage that supports one in all his actions, which comes through the Father within each one of us as we follow our guidance. When one has given himself to God, then there is nothing for him to fear, as the Spirit of God guides and strengthens him in all his actions. I felt strength, love and peace as I rode the colt into Jerusalem. There was nothing for me to fear. I only regretted that the Jewish rulers had closed their minds to my teaching. They would suffer much before they learned to look for God within and express God love for mankind. This was a glorious day for me and one in which God was glorified through me and my actions.

EASTER

As you know, this Sunday commemorates a special event for me. The successful completion of Spiritualizing my body and raising it to express Conscious Oneness with God. But first it (body) had to be healed. This is true of all resurrections that take place in the daily life of each individual, as challenges of health, feelings of lack, insecurity, loneliness, hate or condemnation, as well as all other negative emotions and states of mind that occur and are overcome or dissolved. If these emotions are prolonged, the body is damaged as definitely as though it had been tortured. So a healing of the physical body and also the mind has to take place before the resurrection is completed. This is done through the healing power of God love flowing through the body. The state of mind is healed by the acceptance of the Spirit of God or Christ Spirit. Thus, the whole body and mind is healed and spiritualized and the resurrection is completed. Hallelujah!

Question: Regarding Chas & Myrtle Fillmore

You have had a very interesting evening and a revealing one from Myrtle. Ramel is a member of the Council of Masters and one of the group working here through you. He is just joining us and will have some instruction and teaching to give you. It is possible you will write something with him. Myrtle had grown spiritually since she has been on this side and is working with Masters a great amount of time, even more than Charles. Yes, he is with you quite a bit as he knows you like and teach like he did, and you use his books and teachings.

You are wondering how we (Masters) can remain invisible to Charles and Myrtle. Remember, we are on different planes and yet all planes intermingle, but are not visible to anyone on the individual planes unless it is desired to do so. The Masters can go to each plane. We can go to the astral and etheric planes much easier and at will than we can the earth plane. Souls on the etheric plane can project themselves to the earth plane and go to the astral plane as they desire. Those on the astral plane can only go to the etheric plane. If one is perceptive, he can feel the presence of a soul or Master. I trust this is clear!

Question: Regarding Faith

Faith in action is the only way anything is accomplished. One has to have faith in himself and what he is doing to make any improvement in his life and to manifest the things he desires in his life. When faith is placed in the action of Spirit working in and through oneself, the results are unlimited scope, perfect health, security, freedom from fear, and all negation. Using faith in Spirit as a power to accomplish that which is desired can bring forth anything. It raises the dead, feeds the living with material food as well as spiritual food. Heals the lame, sick, blind and obsessed, builds cities, nations and empires.

When one is filled with faith in Spirit, one can spiritualize one's body and raise it to express Conscious Oneness in God.

We are here with you all the time to assist you in every way we possibly can to help all who call on you. You have been wondering how I (Jesus) can spend so much time here with you and still respond to the many calls for help. It does not matter where I am, as the calls still reach me. And as they (calls) come, I answer each one in thought and consciousness. The Father working through me is limitless and does the work, not me. I just direct it, the same as you do in working with those that call upon you. It would not be feasible for me to go to each one, as they come from all directions and places in the world. Then, too, those Masters working with me assist me in this healing work also. So everyone who calls, is answered in Spirit, just as they are calling in Spirit, and I am free to devote time to the project.

I trust this supplies the answer you needed. You are not taking up my time and causing me to neglect others. The time I spend with you two lovely people is for the good of all mankind as you are the chosen channel through which I and those with me work for humankind. It is true that your outreach is rather limited at this time, but it will continue to grow and expand as you continue teaching. And as soon as the book is published, your outreach will expand to millions. Much more than any other individual's. It is time for you to get ready to be about the Father's business. Will talk to you later. God Bless you both.

Now for the lesson, "God Creates Only Good," which is certainly true, since creation or creating is continual. Were it to cease, the world as well as the universe would also cease to exist. God is continually bringing forth new forms through man's formative power, which is the creative power of God at work in man. Each new child born to woman is a new individual created by God. Each new item brought forth by man has been created by God. Each new animal born to animals is created by God. Each new bird, insect or other form of life is created by God; and this creation continues throughout the universe. Everything God creates is good and only good is created by God.

Every living thing is guided by God to survive, grow and multiply in its environment. That is, every species of insect, reptile, animal, bird, plant, flower, tree, grass, shrub, grains, etc. have all been given the instruction and guidance of God on how to survive and multiply. Furthermore, the survival of each species depends on how each individual species responds to its instinct to live, grow and multiply as well as its reaction to each challenge it meets in its daily life. This includes man.

I will be glad to make some suggestions about the lesson "Fulfillment." This is an excellent topic and one of my favorites. Of course - any topic on Truth is my favorite. Ha! Ha!

The longing soul can only be fulfilled by the recognized and felt presence of God, as the presence of God fulfills the soul's desire for spiritual growth and understanding, and in no other way can it be acquired except through God. The activity of the Spirit of God, the Father, helps the individual feel the Presence and helps him be open and receptive to all guidance leading him to express what he feels in his actions and reactions toward his fellowman. One who feels the Presence of God expresses God love, peace and harmony to all whom he contacts, which is also both seen and felt by all. You might ask, how can you see the God love which is invisible? You can see the results of God love being expressed by an individual in his/her smiling, radiant countenance and hear it in his/her voice, and you can feel the love vibrations coming from him/her. The presence of God certainly fills one and satisfies all of one's corporeal needs as well as one's soul desires. Yes, one is certainly fulfilled through God.

Now, as to Abraham. He reincarnated into another person and as such did come into prominence again, in Biblical times, as a well known character.

Abraham has had several lifetimes since he first died, and is now a Master. As a Master he has a Master's privileges. He can choose to be called whatever name he desires and used in anyone of his incarnations. Thus, he chose the name Abraham, since that is the one he likes the most and was the best liked of those in his many incarnations.

It is not easy to become a Master. But it can be accomplished when the desire is great enough to serve mankind, as you two lovely people have demonstrated and are demonstrating again. You will make it this time around. The men of ancient Biblical times did actually live to be as old as reported. There is really no reason one cannot live as long as one desires in the present body without Spiritualizing it, if one believes one can and eats right and exercises and lets God guide oneself in all that one does. Eventually, an individual would naturally rise to Mastership without seeking it as such. Of course, a person would have to know that his/her body would not grow old, which notion however, is generally accepted these days. Naturally, it is more fulfilling to seek Mastership and also have a young body, in it's prime, with all the advantages of being a Master.

Question: Did you hear Audrés question about people becoming Masters on other planets?

Yes, and it is true that persons on other planets do become Masters. However, just because they are advanced more scientifically than the people on the earth, does not necessarily mean that they are farther advanced spiritually than those on the earth. There are many more facets to the spiritual development of an individual soul than one realizes. This is why it takes so many lifetimes for many souls to advance to the stage of Mastership. Some of the souls that existed in Atlantis are on other planets at this time, drawn there because of the scientific development of those persons or souls there. But they were not spiritually advanced at the time of the Atlantis destruction. In fact, you two lovely people were on Atlantis and worked against some of the souls who were using the spiritual powers they had developed to subjugate mankind.

Thus, it was a selfish purpose, and that is why the land of Atlantis was submerged in the sea. I was there also and knew the two of you when you were killed because of your activities of seeking to teach about one God and using God powers for all mankind and not just a few. We do need workers here, but at this time cannot draw from other planets who are also in need of workers. Even on those planets there are spiritually many who have not sought to become Masters for one reason or another. Principally, because they like it as it is. They can live for long periods of time without becoming Masters, and so are enjoying things as they are. In some cases it is more difficult to get them to change their thinking to become Masters than it is on the earth plane, because they do not have the great incentive to change as do earthbound souls whose lives are not as pleasant and lovely as theirs. We are continually working with them, as we are with souls on the earth plane. Then too, there are separate Master Councils on each planet. But as Masters, we are "inter-changeable" and can work wherever we choose to work in the Universe. We generally choose to work on the planet where we attained Mastership, as we feel closer to mankind on that planet.

"Plan Your Future!" yes, it does take planning to achieve one's goals whatever they are. As you know, I had to train and plan my work and how I would present it to humankind. I had to know myself and my relationship to God and my fellowman. I had to become involved with myself to learn my capabilities to respect myself and to learn to love myself to the degree that I could then express love to all mankind. Remember, you can only see in others that which is in you.

You can only give to others that which you have to give. Therefore, if we are going to give and express God love to mankind, we have to develop it in ourselves. The same with all of the attributes or powers within. They are there, but must be developed through expressing and using them. Through practice, prayer and meditation we develop and strengthen our twelve powers. Then we must bring these forth into manifestation by using them. So know what your goal is - to express the perfection of the indwelling Christ in the outer. Then through prayer and meditation let God guide you in bringing forth the manifestation of your goal. "Plan your Future - work with your plan to attain your highest goal." In doing so, you are also becoming involved with other people by sharing your Truth with them, where and when they need it. This multiplies your powers and develops them faster.

Question: Any comment on "Let's Be A Blessing?"

First, to be a blessing one must express and radiate love, God love, to all with whom one comes into contact with during one's daily living. An individual expresses this God love by being thoughtful, considerate, and helpful the best he/she knows. God love is expressed by being considerate of other people's feelings and desires, as well as being polite and generous in giving of one's goodwill, cheerfulness, joy and enthusiasm. Furthermore, by being thoughtful and seeking ways in which another can be blessed by giving service, such as teaching Truth to those who are seeking relief from their negative results. Also, to speak words of Truth to anyone reacting negatively to any situation or condition, as well as being helpful, whenever possible, in assisting others in performing their daily task, whatever it may be. To smile is to express God love. To encourage, praise and give thanks is also to express God love. To give a soft, loving reply to harsh words as well as to be patient, peaceful and kind is to express God love. Yes, expressing the love and peace of God means being a blessing to the world. Only then will there be peace when everyone learns to express it.

Question: Regarding Joseph

Yes, Jim, Joseph was one of my incarnations and, as you know, a most interesting man. I am glad to have had the life of Joseph since it helped me rise in spiritual awareness of my true self, as I let the Spirit guide me in all I did as Joseph. I was in my right place at that time regarding my growth and development. Each and every individual soul has certain things it has to learn to develop to the full expression of God. In addition, each incarnation is entered into in order to learn or accomplish certain things. Just as you and Audre came into this lifetime to learn certain things you needed to know for your spiritual development and also to rid yourselves of certain things that were holding back the realization of your true Self. You were also to help us in acquainting mankind of the actions taken to enter the New Age now coming into manifestation.

You are right about the statements purportedly made by me (Jesus) regarding Satan or the Devil. I did not use those terms, as I knew then and still know, that there is no such thing as the Devil or Satan. This is only something invented by man as an excuse for doing that which he knows he should not do. Temptations can be likened to Satan or the Devil, but only as symbols of error thinking and desires that seemingly need to be satisfied. We sometimes disregard our spiritual needs in favor of our sensual desires and spend time and energy striving to satisfy a want that is a passing fancy and only temporal at that. Such desires supposedly originate from the so-called Devil.

"Imbued With Power"

Very few persons are truly using all the power with which they are imbued for their highest good, as most do not realize they have this power to use daily, even momentarily, in their living. The power with which every soul is imbued is God Power. The very creative power of God is implanted in each and every individual and is the power used in daily activities, whether or not one realizes he/she is using it, or even has it. How the individual is using this power can be determined by the results in his/her life. The way the power is used is determined by knowledge of it, mental attitude and desire expressing through them to will to do. A Master and a servant can have the same knowledge. But the mental attitude of a Master and a servant determines how the knowledge is used. And a desire for good directs the will which directs the power in its activity.

Audré asked about Asenath and whether or not she was one of Miriam's incarnations and the answer is yes, she was. She was my wife then and for the final time prior to us becoming Masters. So you see it happens to all of us.

Our soulmates do come together at various times and usually more frequently as we progress spiritually toward our goal of attaining Mastership, whether or not we are aware of our goal. At the present time, not many are aware of the presence of the Spiritualized Earth Plane and the Masters. That is another reason why it is imperative to get the book on the market so that as many people as possible can become aware of their highest goal - Mastership.

Question: Regarding Beards and Shaving

Yes, men shaved with sharp knives and some beards were plucked out so facial beard would not grow. Not all men wore beards and long hair as we did during our ministry.

"Free To Be Oneself"

Very few persons are truly expressing their true Self. We are "Free to Be Oneself," but just what is oneself? Oneself is one's God Self or Christ Self which is the pattern of the God Idea of perfect man, that is to be manifested in the outer world of today. It is to be done NOW! and not at some future date in some far-off heaven after one dies, as has been taught and still is preached in some churches. Each individual is free to travel at his own pace to accomplish this manifestation. The only pressure that is brought to bear on him to cause him to do this, is his own feeling or desire to do so, which is his indwelling Christ urging him to seek the better life that is his and to stop limiting himself. To go forth seeking his highest good in all he sees and feels, knowing that his true guidance comes from within himself and is the true Self he is to express in the manifest world.

"Come Unto Me"

The title "Come Unto Me" intrigues me (Jesus) and should for all who attend the service tomorrow. When I said this to those who were listening to me, I was trying to tell them that they were to stop struggling, straining and striving to obtain their living. That in doing so they were just burdening themselves with useless strife and worry, unhappiness, illness, fears, jealousy, inharmony and feelings of lack and desperation. All of which tear down the body and nervous system and lead to further excesses in drinking and various kinds of drugs. Yes, in those days there were various kinds of drugs available to those who desired them. The Chinese have used Opium for many thousands of years, and other countries also have their alcoholic beverages and drugs. All of these things can be avoided or dissolved by seeking the Christ within and letting the Spirit of God carry the load and guide one to his/her highest good. The only requirement or so-called "yoke" is to put God first in one's life, and in prayer as well as meditation go within seeking oneness with the Christ or Father, and become a willing channel for God to express through. All God powers will then be yours to use in your daily living, just as I used them and still do.

As for your question whether Daniel was one of my incarnations, since he was so much like Joseph, the answer is yes. Daniel was a real character just as Joseph was, and it was a beautiful life as a result of trusting in the Father and letting Him guide me in all I did. It was another stepping stone to my incarnation as Jesus. The fiery furnace incident actually took place and my three friends demonstrated the protecting God power in which we all live, but do not realize it. We do not use it to help ourselves as we could.

"The fiery furnace" is indeed the world of materiality in which we can become so involved that we neglect our spiritual nature, and our true inner Self becomes entombed in the material world and atrophies because it is not developed. When this happens, our lives are unhappy and we are subject to the ills of the world. It is only when we seek to know God and express our God-like attributes that our lives are opened to the glory of God and we have the unending bliss of eternal love, happiness, peace, harmony, life, health and abundant supply of all the good we could ever desire. Only one's spiritual power expressing through one's actions and reactions can overcome the trials and tribulations of the material world. The power of the I AM, the Christ within each individual is all the power one needs to overcome anything. The I AM, the Christ will overcome the might of manpower and cause it to fail. You can say that the test in the fiery furnace will prove whether one is serving God or Mammon. Look at your life and you be the judge.

"The True Kingdom" is a good one. And since you have worked on the dream interpretation, I shall confine my remarks to the "Stone Not Made With Hands." As Daniel has said, this represents the 5th kingdom or state of mind of the individual. As he/she increases in spiritual understanding and wisdom, he/she realizes the folly of giving importance to satisfying materialistic, sensual and selfish desires, and seeking to fill his/her life with them. They are temporal, and will disappear in a relatively short time. They are things you cannot take with you when you separate your soul from your body. These are the things that can be taken from you by a thief or immoral person. Only the Truth of God is permanent and God love, peace, happiness, joy, strength, power, health, will, zeal, wisdom and other spiritual attributes are your wealth and sustaining legacy from God your Father. These are of God and the other things are man made items that are truly worthless in a spiritual world. Meditation and prayer are the stepping stones to the true kingdom of God which we all desire to share and may, when we learn to accept and use Truth principles in our daily living.

"The Lion's Den" does represent unregenerate thoughts and feelings that have gained strength through man's continual thinking of them and arousing fears and doubts regarding his good in material ways, as well as doubting his own spiritual strength and understanding. Man is in the "Lion's Den" of how he lets material and finite things be his goal in life and therefore lets them control his thoughts and consequently dictate his actions. Darius represents the human will in a strong and domineering way. However, he does recognize that there is a higher power than he is, thus he sets Daniel higher than the rest of the material thoughts and desires represented by the satrap and other officials. Thoughts of resentment, criticism, condemnation, doubts and fears can be changed by higher spiritual thoughts, prayers and following the guidance of God. This is the demonstration of Daniel. It is a beautiful story and one that makes a point for all to understand.

"The Handwriting On The Wall"

The handwriting does say, as you have decided, that if one does not turn from living in a materialistic way of trying to satisfy his sensual desires, to the realization of God being the One power and presence in his life, he will come to an unpleasant end of his life on the earth plane due to his way of thinking and acting. By acting thus, he has been found wanting in his expression of his Christ Self by misusing his God-given spiritual powers. The handwriting is sure, and prophecies truly. As the law of cause and effect is immutable, these prohecies based on its outcome can be considered true. When an individual realizes that God is the One presence and power in his/her life, then that life will become glorious indeed.

"The World Can Be Changed."

This is a true statement since man formed it as it is and anything man forms he can change to be like he wishes by changing his thinking and acting. You also know, that man strives for peace, but does not realize he must first change his thoughts from resentment, hate, envy, greed, criticism, fear and desires for sensual satisfaction and passion, to thoughts of love, peace, harmony, faith, joy, happiness, abundance, and a willingness to help and encourage his fellowman. The law of cause and effect will guarantee the results.

You asked where the astral and etheric planes are. They are near the earth plane. The astral plane touches the earth plane and is where the so-called earth-bound souls stay until they are ready to go to the etheric plane to prepare for their future life on the earth plane. The etheric plane is higher in the atmosphere, out of the pattern of traffic in the air. In a way, both planes are intermingled with the earth plane. The souls pass easily from one to the other whenever they desire to do so. Each soul is completely free to pursue its own spiritual place and method of expressing its spiritual understanding as long as it has not committed some depraved atrocity on the earth plane. In that case, the soul is taken to another planet to learn among others of its own level of spiritual understanding which may be nil or very low. It is a very rough existence and these souls will grow together.

"That Your Joy May Be Made Full."

This is a quote from the Bible which I am supposed to have stated during my ministry. I probably did, as I taught to be cheerful even under adverse conditions and optimistic rather than pessimistic, as well as to look for and to see the good in all persons and situations. It is a joy to the heart of the beholder and a fulfillment of one's good to the cheerful individual. Joy is an attitude of mind that stems from one's confidence in his/her own self to think, act and achieve under all circumstances. This state of mind is achieved by going within to the indwelling Christ and submitting one's mind, heart and soul to God; seeking guidance to one's highest good. Then one can go forth following his guidance with a sense of peace, confidence and a feeling of pure joy that all is well with him and his world. This is heaven on earth and is that which most persons are seeking; peace of mind and heart as well as an assurance that good is forthcoming in divine order.

The mountain represents spiritual understanding which is obscured or unperceived by the individual because of his interest in and commitment to material things and activities to the extent that he has more or less closed his mind to spiritual ideas and thoughts. This is true of most individuals throughout the world at the present time. Thus, it is necessary to remind all who will listen, that their lives will be easier, happier, healthier and more joyful when they turn to God and let the Father God be an active partner in their lives. Tell them about the ultimate goal that is attained when one reaches the mountain top of Mastership in God.

What a beautiful ideal to strive for, and it is not out of reach for any individual in this lifetime. It is a beautiful concept that may be too incredible for most individuals to believe, but if one or two will accept it and only try to believe, it will manifest.

When you tell someone to "Behold The Christ" in another person or themselves, many do not know just what you mean or refer to. Of course, we know that we are referring to the Christ Spirit within each and every individual. In first Genesis, in the part about the creation of man, it refers to the image or likeness of God implanted in man. Possibly more important than this, is to help everyone see that within every person there is good. Whether or not it is being expressed in their ulterior way of life. In a way, the word God is a contraction of the word "Good" because GOD IS GOOD. All of the good in the universe is God. Good is an expression of God or you may say, God expresses in and through man as good works, thinking and speaking.

Question: What comment do you have on the woman's statement under hypnosis that she saw you stop the stoning of Mary Magdalene? This differs from the account in the Bible and in your books which says that Mary was brought to you to see what you would say.

That is a very interesting article that you have read. As I recall it, the young woman was brought to me to see what I had to say about the stoning in an effort to discredit me and my teaching. As I gave it in my story, the young woman was not hurt except for the manhandling she endured, and not from any rocks. The woman could have misread, or rather misunderstood what was going on and thought she was being stoned instead of being hurt by the rough handling. I certainly would have known if she had been hit by stones. Otherwise, her account was fairly accurate. I did not say that anyone who had not lain with her cast the first stone, but said what I put in the book. She could have misunderstood. I do not remember her at this time. We possibly should give more detail in the account of this incident. There are some other things that should be revised also.

"God Needs You"

It is a good subject and one that more ministers should talk about and emphasize. Each individual must eventually learn to realize that he/she is a channel through which God expresses. God can only express through mankind and only to the extent man permits, or is open and receptive to the guidance of God. As the individual is open and receptive to the guidance of his/her inner Spirit, he/she expresses God in manifestation outwardly and in various forms. All of the misery, powerty, sickness, fear, war, murders, rape, cruelty, torture, pillaging, rioting, violent dissenting and other disruptions and destructive actions are the result of individuals closing their minds and hearts to the plan of God love, peace and guidance. Those committing such acts will suffer the consequences of their foolishness. The law of cause and effect is immutable and will exact a tenfold payment in return. Any punishment by authorities is only part of the payment that will be exacted. Thus, God needs the compliance of every person who is willing to be a channel of expressing love and peace to all those with closed minds. Such love and peace expressed to the world will eventually dissolve all ill-will and anger to manifest peace throughout the world. We here on this Spiritualized earth plane are doing what we can to guide man to his highest good, but it takes people there in your earth plane to set the example and to lead and guide all persons to accepting God's guidance. As you know, this is the purpose of our project which is not yet off the ground.

Question: Brother, can you tell us if there were really two tablets of stone which the ten commandments were written on? If so, how and who wrote on them?

Yes, I can tell you what you want to know about the stones or tablets on which the ten commandments were written. There were actually two pieces of stone that were engraved with the commandments and other rules and regulations. These were God-inspired writings that would let the people know what they are to do or not to do. The writings were done by Moses on the mountain, much like John. There are other instances in which Masters or those close to becoming Masters can do such work.

"Be A Good Receiver," is an interesting subject and one I like to talk about. In order for anyone to receive the good they are entitled to and desire, they have to first be a good receiver, that is, ready for their good and able to handle it when it arrives. To be a good receiver, one has to expect it and be prepared to act or use it as soon as received. One has to have faith that it is coming from the One Source and will arrive as expected. One should make plans on how the good will be utilized for the benefit of all concerned. While preparing for the good and then upon receipt of the good, one should discuss it only with those directly involved with it. Thus, negative vibrations will not be drawn toward it and dissipate the power within it. Our Father God is the source as well as the good, therefore one might say, He has given to himself and to all who will accept it. In order to be able to accept, an individual has to be ready to receive his/her good and not block it off with negation.

Now for your lesson entitled **"Now Is The Time."** This is a good title and one that I like to talk about. There is no time like the present time, and is the only time one has which he can call his own. This minute we are using right now is the only minute we have. The one that was just finished is gone, never to return, used up and cannot be recalled nor lived over. The one coming has not arrived as yet and only has a promise, it cannot be used until it arrives and then only fleetingly. So, the only time we can control how we use, is the one we have right now. Actually, there is no assurance that the next minute will be ours to use as we see fit. The only way we can be sure that we have control of our life and the time we desire to use, is when we are expressing Conscious Oneness with God as Masters in Him. Otherwise we are subject to the vagaries of time as applied through the material-minded individual. He who turns to God and seeks to express the Christ ideas of perfect man is on the path to complete control of himself and all elements around him. Each step up brings him closer to the goal. So NOW is the time to turn within.

It is most certainly a "Moment of Truth," when one contacts his/her indwelling Higher Self. A feeling of oneness and happiness pervades the entire being as one feels the presence of God within him/herself. A feeling of confidence and strength that one can accomplish all that needs to be accomplished at any time. There is only one way to do this and it is through the giving of oneself to God in complete submission. The gift of oneself to God brings immediate rewards in health, happiness and prosperity, never before manifested in one's life. This is the true giving that opens the channel to God's gift of love and peace. There is no higher or richer reward. It cannot be purchased with a coin or in any other way.

Now, for your question regarding the death penalty. Actually, the death penalty for a convicted murderer, or one who has committed a particularly vicious crime, is a fair penalty since it is the result of the Law of Cause and Effect. Thus, what you told your afternoon class is true, that a soul that had been separated from its body as a result of such a sentence, or some other action, would be removed from this (earth) planet to another, where like souls were living. In such a place, the violent souls can work out their own salvation and soul growth together, without hurting the more peaceful souls. What is actually occurring now is that all souls that are more or less violently inclined and show no signs of desiring to change are being removed from this planet to another more suited to their talents and desires. In this way, the more spiritual-minded souls can form a more spiritually oriented world in the coming Aquarian Age.

Your title, **"No Fear In Love,"** is a good one filled with Truth. Love is filled with power that can dissolve all negation when it is properly applied to any individual or situation. Love is the most powerful force that is expressed by God through man. All love expressed by man is God inspired even though it may be perverted in expression by man's selfish desire for physical rather than spiritual fulfillment. When God comes first in a couple's life, love can be expressed in a physical way with both physical and spiritual desires fulfilled beautifully. When an individual is expressing God love to all humankind there is no room for fears or doubts since these have been dissolved.

Fears and doubts appear when criticism, envy, greed, hate, condemnation and deceit are permitted to reign in an individual's consciousness and is being expressed only partially. But when love is released, all negative thoughts and feelings disappear and love reigns supreme. Then the individual is filled with joy, happiness, health, vitality and energy.

For your information, when I said one is to "become like children to enter the kingdom of heaven," I meant that one is to accept the teaching that God Is Love unequivocally and whole heartedly, and step out in faith, knowing that one will be led to his/her highest good. In this concept there is freedom from all fear, worry and feelings of lack. One is happy, healthy, prosperous, joyous and filled with the love for his fellow human. An individual loves his neighbor and does all he can to make his life the same. This is the only way one can be truly open and receptive to The Father's guidance in all one thinks, says and does. This then becomes the True Path to the Kingdom of God.

Now for the lesson on **"Re-Creation."** This is the ultimate goal of every individual to re-create his entire being into the original Spiritual being that he was created to express, but strayed away from doing. Nearly every individual alive today and manifesting on the Earth plane is existing or living in an imbalanced consciousness, unless he is a Master. If the individual were not imbalanced, he would be a Master expressing Conscious Oneness with God. In order to attain a perfectly balanced consciousness, one must let his Spiritual nature express itself in the outer in tune with all other phases of his nature.

When this is accomplished, man has time for work that is performed with enthusiasm, joy and expediency, as well as recreation, which is done in moderation and for the purpose of relaxing and renewing the nervous system. There must also be time for family and, of course, time to share one's life, love and self-expression of the Christ Self with God. This gradually evolves into Mastership, which is man's ultimate goal. So, this is in Truth to Re-create a new life in God.

Praise and Giving Thanks is, and was one of my favorite topics. I (Jesus) taught that one should pray, giving thanks for the receipt of one's desire before receiving it, as evidence of faith in God as the source of all good, and that it would therefore be supplied.

The Transforming Power is love; God love. Personal love, is an expression of God love personified, and in some instances downgraded to a form of lust and passion. But nevertheless, it is an expression, in some degree, of God love. God love transforms the meanest man, woman or beast to a living and tender individual, willing to give of itself to the utmost. It was God love that I (Jesus) used to dissipate the storm, heal the sick, raise the dead and all the other things done by me. All this was accomplished through the use of God love power. It is God love that will transform this world of turmoil and turbulence into a world of peace. And it is God love, being expressed through man, that will accomplish this.

God love has to be expressed through one human to another. It comes from within and flows outwardly from each individual.

Oh yes, LOVE is a universal power that flows throughout the universe, but it has to be absorbed or taken into the individual's heart and then expressed from within outwardly.

Give of yourself. This is what I (Jesus) taught as love and compassion. This is what I demonstrated as the way to express Oneness with God. One has to give himself to God and let himself be guided in how he is to serve God. An individual serves God, when he/she is kind, generous, helpful, considerate and loving. Thus, he helps his friends, neighbors and family to understand their relationship to God and their fellowman. This, you both know and are demonstrating to the best of your abilities and spiritual understanding.

Question: Were you Joshua also?

I believe that once before I told you I was Joseph, Joshua, Daniel, and Elisha prior to the present incarnation of Jesus. In each incarnation I had different duties and yet each helped me reach my present attainment of Mastership. You and Audre have been in nearly every one of my incarnations also, and you knew and worked with me in one way or another. In each of these incarnations you too have grown, just as you are both growing now. You have had more incarnations since then, and are now in a position where you can become Masters.

"In The Beginning - God," in which you intend to show that each one is to bring God into his/her life and consciousness at the beginning of the New Year, so as to have a good year and achieve the goals he/she desires. This is an excellent idea and is based on the story of Caleb and Joshua as spies in the Promised Land, and is sound and good. To enter any endeavor with the assurance that God is in charge of one's life and affairs will be a means of sure success. Faith in God gives courage, confidence and strength to overcome and rise above any challenge one may encounter.

"Prepare For An Exciting Year," is a good title for the first Sunday of the year and is well chosen to help all who accept it to have a good year; one of the best of their lives. As you have planned, they are to enter this New Year with the right attitude of mind, by letting God guide them in all they think, say and do. This is the only way to a truly exciting year. To not know what is coming is exciting enough, but to know that only good is on its way makes it even more exciting. The anticipation and expectancy of good and only good coming makes it certain that good is being manifest as it comes in an orderly way and is increasingly manifesting your highest good.

Now for Bishop Patrick. He is an excellent psychic. He can and does help many people who believe in him. He is working with entities on the astral and etheric planes, and good is being done. As far as we know, there are no real Masters working with the Bishop. Some entities do call themselves Masters, but they are not of the White Brotherhood, as we are. Neither are they on this spiritualized earth plane.

It is wise to plan for what you want, so the Father can help bring it forth through you. This is the power you are speaking of. To bring it forth you must know what it is you desire and that it is for your highest good, for it to be truly beneficial. Sometimes we desire that which is not for our highest good and when it comes forth, we are disappointed or in difficulty because it is in our life. So we do have to use wisdom and good judgement in using the unlimited powers we have to bring forth that which is for our highest good and for all those concerned in it with us. I used this power to heal, raise the dead, feed the multitudes and to Spiritualize my body and raise it to express Conscious Oneness with God, as a Master. There is no limit to what can be brought forth with it. But if it is not used for the highest good of all concerned, then disastrous results come from its use to the detriment of the user. This is a built-in feature since it is God power and is to be used only for the good of mankind and not in a selfish way to gain power over humankind. The Atlanteans tried this and learned it does not work that way.

As I (Jesus) always thought and taught, that one should be filled with the joy of God and go forth with enthusiasm and joy, ready to accomplish all that needs to be done. This, because when a person is filled with the love, strength and wisdom of God, he is being guided to his highest good as he follows his inner guidance. One who lives in the described manner becomes filled with assurance, confidence and a joyful heart. This kind of an individual can conquer the world and do whatever he desires to do. He is letting the power of God work in and through him, guiding him to his highest good in an easy way.

Your lesson of "Unity - The Way Up," is a most appropriate one for this day and time. There are so many ways in which unity in an individual's life is necessary for spiritual growth. And unity in marriage is necessary for a happy expression of God love between husband and wife as well as the rest of the family. Furthermore, unity between neighbors, friends, towns, cities, states and nations is vital to spiritual and material growth. In fact, there has to be unity throughout the universe, or chaos would result. However, this all begins with the individual who has to have unity within himself. That means, he must establish the right relationship within himself, between his spiritual and material self. The inner and the outer must also be in a proper balance, to achieve one's goal of Mastership.

Question: Brother, do you wish to answer our question about another sister of Mary and Martha's, named Ruth? Is this true? Also, what about the things Joseph Smith wrote in his "Book of Mormon," and other information?

Yes, I will tell you that there was another sister of Lazarus whose name was Ruth. She was never mentioned, as she did not enter into our friendship or into the action of Christianity until after I had left the Apostles. She came later to try to help the loyal followers in the commune. She was married and living in another community than Bethany. She did leave her family, to live with the Believers, but later returned to them. I knew her, but not as intimately as I did Lazarus, Mary and Martha.

Now, about the claims of Joseph Smith. I did not appear in a vision to him nor would it be possible for God to have made such an appearance, as he (Smith) says happened. He may have had such a vision in a dream, but to my knowledge no Master did as he (Smith) claimed. Certainly John the Baptist did not, because he no longer exists since Elijah resumed his appearance as himself and let the form of John the Baptist return to nothingness from which it came. After all, John was a necessary character in a drama which Elijah agreed to play or depict. There is no John the Baptist soul in existence. I have asked Peter, James and John, who are here, and each said they were not the ones who came to Joseph Smith and the others. Some spiritually oriented souls or entities may have been the ones who appeared and helped those people, leading them closer to their Christ Selves.

By the way, I did not teach baptism by immersion in water. It is not necessary. I have taught that spiritual baptism is by the indwelling Christ Spirit, and does not come through water or any outer vehicle or method.

For quite awhile after leaving the Apostles in their country to find their own true Christ Self and go forth to teach that which I had taught them; I made use of my ability to go where I wished and to appear either visible or invisible. Thus, I visited various parts of the world to teach and demonstrate the Truth to all who would listen. As you know, there are traces of many peoples around the earth that were far advanced and who did many wonderful things.

Each individual must realize and express the Christ Self in the outer. The Christ within is the pattern of that which each one of us has to express. It took me (Jesus) some time to realize this Truth. I called it the Father, as I realized that the source of power, God Power, is within me and every person alike. This is the Christ, the I AM, or whatever you or anyone else wants to call it. This is the source of all power an individual needs in order to accomplish all he/she is to do. It is the source of power which enabled me to do all that I did and is the reason I said, that you are to do the works I did and even greater works than these. This is true today and will be in the future. "I AM THE CHRIST," is a fact of each individual and is an accurate description of his true inner self which he must and will eventually express in his ulterior life. If not in this lifetime then further down the line in another life. Man/woman has all eternity (to accomplish this).

"By Our Love," is a good title and gives me the thought that it is by our love that we accomplish all good things. All our greatest efforts are spurred by some phase of love. Love of or desire for things cause us to increase our efforts to obtain money to buy them. It is love of mankind that causes us to do something for its good. It is love that causes us to seek a mate. There are many ways in which one can express love for one's fellowman. Kindness, encouragement, unselfishness, cheerfulness, helpfulness, forgiveness, patience, understanding, thoughts of peace, respect, and all others are forms of love.

The title "For Us or Against Us," is a provocative one. Of course we know that God does not take sides for or against anyone. God is neither for nor against someone or something. If that were true, then God would be limited by limiting thoughts and ideas. God is Good; all the good there is. God is Love. God is wisdom and all other wonderful attributes combined into one Creative Power that is to be expressed through humankind. It is the only channel for truly expressing God in all phases of Creative Power. Since man can think, and has free will to do as he sees fit, therefore God can only express through man as man lets the expression come forth into manifestation. By using the Creative Power within himself, man expresses God according to his spiritual awareness or development. He does the best he knows how, as his spiritual growth permits him to. He cannot be or do something that is not in accord with his self-image, which includes his acceptance of the divine laws of behavior and activity under all circumstances. Thus, man can and does use his God Power to the best of his present ability.

We will now talk about your lesson for tomorrow, "A Time for Growth." This is a very timely lesson on Lent and how much it can mean to each individual who observes it with prayer and seeking spiritual understanding through meditation and fasting from negative thinking, speaking and acting. This will help dissolve all negation that is manifesting in one's life, and form a life filled with peace love, prosperity, health and happiness. The period of forty days only, represents a period of purification and cleansing of negative beliefs, fears, thoughts and actions from one's life. In actuality, it could be forty minutes, hours, days, weeks, months or years, depending on how much negation there would be to dissolve and the intent and sincerity of the individual. A period of fasting can be very enlightening and allows the Spirit more freedom to flow through the individual, bringing forth spiritual growth, expansion and a general feeling of well-being never previously felt. It is a wonderful feeling that can only be achieved through spiritual growth and understanding with a closer feeling of oneness with the Father-God.

You have to learn to do these things for yourself. Oh, we help, but as I did after the crucifixion, I had to open myself to the Healing Power of the Father and let it flow through me. There was a period of several hours that elapsed before Elijah and Moses arrived to help me. This is the way it was. I had to do the big part myself, then they helped.

We Masters can do some, but you have to do most of it yourself. This may seem strange to you at this time, but you will recognize the logic and Truth of it in the future. In lower stages of spiritual development where people believe in outside help as the Healing Power, they are receiving healings that are more or less temporary, but nevertheless, they have received a little spiritual growth, as a result.

The title "Inner Altar," is well chosen, since you already have in mind that it is the place within each individual where the Son of God, the Christ lives and directs the activities of the individual to the extent that it is permitted to do so. The "Inner Altar" is the place one enters in order to truly worship God, the Christ, the Father, as I (Jesus) called it, and it can only do for a person that which can be done through the person.

If an individual is not open and receptive, then the Christ Spirit will not force Itself upon the individual. Thus, the soul loses the opportunity, at that time, to express the Christ as much as it is rightfully due him/her.

"Look Up and Behold the Good." I will share some thoughts with you on beholding the good. As you know, I (Jesus) believe and taught in beholding the good in all things. This is the only way you can rise above any seeming adverse happenings or circumstances. Nothing happens by accident, as there is a definite cause to trigger or start every effect. The effect is then developed and grows, or is dissolved by the way it is received by the individual. The individual uses his power of imagination to bring forth into manifestation those things, ideas, feelings and emotions he has deep within himself. Consequently, the kind of life a person will have depends on what he holds in his mind and heart. It should be emphasized that he can change his life anytime he chooses to. Thus, a human has been given complete dominion over his life, affairs, and circumstances in which he lives. He is using his God-given power to form his life and he alone is responsible for it. Of course, he has all eternity to manifest the true state of perfection that he is supposed to bring forth.

Now, for my part to that which we will talk about; the book of my supposedly secret doctrines which you already have put down on paper in book form, as well as all that I (Jesus) taught during my earthly ministry. There was no secret group to whom I taught, other than the twelve disciples. Of course, much of the time there were those who followed us and joined in on our discussions. I did not enlarge on this in my book, but could do so if we felt it necessary. An example of those who studied with us are the seventy I sent out. Now, these were close followers who demonstrated their acceptance of the Truth, as I taught it. They did not continue, nor were they a part of any so-called secret group. There were such groups formed later on, after I no longer actively led them in person, since I made my final appearance on the earth plane some five or six months after the crucifixion. If I had stayed longer the work would not have been done nor progressed as it did. The disciples and others would have continued to lean on, or depend on me and not their own inner Christ Self. This is the most important part of my teaching that each individual must learn to manifest his own God-given powers and express his Christ Self.

"Sharing Is Growing," is a good title for a needed lesson to many in your congregation. The parable of the talents certainly describes the necessary action as well as the result of correct action, or lack of it. We give of ourselves, our love, strength, wisdom, kindness, compassion, understanding, and other God-given attributes to help others in various ways. We can give money, but with it we must give love, or it becomes not the real blessing it is supposed to be. One cannot rest on one's laurels of the past because this begins to stagnate and deteriorate, and neither grows nor increases. Good deeds and acts truly come to life by being consistently applied. Through such practice, the giver will receive rewards far beyond his/her expectation. When an individual gives of himself, there is the experience of increase rather than decrease. Only by not giving does a person experience decrease.

"Forgiveness Releases," is a Truth statement. When one forgives, one is free of all limitations and becomes then open and receptive to God love. A feeling of unforgiveness blocks the flow of God love and all good from coming to a person. An individual cannot express love from the heart when there is a feeling of unforgiveness and resentment. In the scripture story of my attending a dinner given by a Pharisee who did not accord me the curtesy, of that time, by washing my feet or having them washed by a servant, was in a direct sense an insult. However, I held no rancor toward him for the neglect. I knew there was a studied reason behind such an act. When the woman cleansed my feet with her tears of repentance and dried them with her hair, she was giving herself to God and resolving to lead a new life. Thus, she had in a sense sought God for forgiveness and received it in her heart. She forgave herself and changed her life. This is true forgiveness in action. She was truly free and absolved of all so-called sin. This is what I meant when I told her to go in peace. She had raised or saved herself by her repentance and forgiveness.

I realize there are times you rather doubt if it is truly I, Jesus of Nazareth, who is doing this writing. Therefore, you can hardly be critical of those who cannot conceive of the fact, let alone the idea of me doing this with you. As I have said, in time they will believe when you are able to make demonstrations. You are getting closer and better every day. Stay with us and you both will benefit greatly.

"Our Responsibility." This is a good subject and one that I believe in and taught as well as demonstrated during my last ministry on the earth plane. You are right in thinking that each individual bears the responsibility of using his/her Spiritual Powers and attributes to glorify God, the Father, rather than himself, or to spend his inheritance on trash, just as the Prodigal Son story illustrates. At the present time, the majority of humankind is not using their Spiritual Powers to attain their highest goal or to even help their fellow human to an appreciable degree. Only when an emergency arises is man stirred out of his self-preoccupation and then, only temporarily, to give some money or a little time. We have been given the power to rise above all negation and to help others do so. But seemingly we neglect to use the power, or use it incorrectly, so as to bring negation in our lives. By using the wisdom and faith God has endowed us with, can we do all things to bring forth our highest good. It is time, that every man, woman and child be committed to God and his work, to bring forth into manifestation the perfect world - sharing God love, peace and happiness.

(Palm Sunday) "Inner Light." This lesson is a good one, and should encourage all who hear it to use the power of their Inner Christ Self, which lights their way, to rise above challenges, just as I did on that day when I entered Jerusalem. It had a double effect or meaning. First, it was a triumphal entry in that it showed the leaders of the Jews that the people liked my works and were supporting me. Of course, the people did think I would be their king because despite my teaching and works they thought of me as an earthly king and not as a true spiritual leader. The second effect was, that it enraged the Jewish leaders and goaded them to take the action I wanted them to take. My time had come to make the final demonstration and they had to bring it about. The Christ within me was guiding me to do all I was to do. This is the Inner Light that lights the way for every individual who lets his true Christ Self be in charge of his life.

You have in mind some good ideas to express the Truth that I demonstrated and taught, leading to the climax of the resurrection. Everything I taught and demonstrated was, in fact, a step toward the ultimate goal of resurrecting the body and soul, combining them with the Spirit of God to express the perfection of God. This is what each and every soul will ultimately do and each one has the power, knowledge, wisdom, strength, and faith to raise his body and soul to express oneness with God in this lifetime, if he desires to do so, and strong enough to try. If he tries, he will be helped by Masters who are ever ready to help those seeking spiritual upliftment and growth. The Spirit of God within each individual is the strength one uses to grow. It is up to the individual, since no one can do it for him. Not even God.

You have been asking, what is meant by giving yourself to God? It means that one surrenders himself to the Spirit of God within himself and seeks the guidance of Spirit in everything one thinks, says and does. This is seeking the Kingdom of God and its righteousness or right thinking. When one does this he is led to his highest good and develops himself, as he follows his calling to express that which the Father guides him to express. He is thus tuned in to Infinite wisdom, power, strength, joy, happiness, health, and love. Yes, Peace Pilgrim is a good example of giving oneself to God and following the calling received.

As we have said, the animal souls and the human souls do not transmigrate into other bodies, but always into the rightful body line. You know about the human soul and its destination. The animal soul does grow and expand to a highly evolved spiritual understanding and eventually enjoys life with the Masters or highly evolved souls on the etheric plane. Some animal souls that do not evolve spiritually, just as some human souls do not choose to grow, will be together with those human souls like them, either on the earth plane or some other planet in the universe, which is of the right consciousness to receive them. It is conceivable that a time will come when the human souls have all achieved Mastership. Then the animal souls will also have achieved their highest development and they will all be together, living in the harmonious Spiritualized earth plane. This, of course, is the ultimate goal of all souls in the universe. There is all eternity to consummate the plan, which is what we are all working for and toward.

The question raised about baptism was answered in that I, did most of the baptizing spiritually. We were seldom in a place where there was water. But when we were, and the persons to be baptized wanted the water, we used it. Then the disciples began baptizing, using the spiritual method and water, if desired. In reality, it makes little difference which method is used or both, as long as the acceptance of the Spirit of God comes from within and not in intellectual expression solely to impress others. It is the baptism of spirit that is important.

I heard Audré's request for a simple explanation of the Passover and its true meaning metaphysically. Actually, blood on the gateposts represents the Life, the Spirit of God, being ever ready to enter one's life as one is open and receptive to it. As an individual opens his mind and heart to the inspiration and guidance, his "first born spiritual thoughts and inspiration" will be "saved" from destruction or dissolution by negative or error beliefs and concepts. Also, one's spiritual understanding will increase much more quickly. By using spiritual words and ideas in one's daily living, spiritual growth will be much faster. This is the meaning of fasting, scriptural quotes etc, to one's forehead as well as otherwise holding them in one's mind. Of course, the Jews do not regard it in this manner, but in a more orthodox way, as in the Bible, and by celebrating Passover, which is a form of thanksgiving for their well-being and growth.

Question: Brother, what about souls? We say souls have always been. We also say God is continually creating in the universe. Does this include souls as being continually created by God?

That is a good question and the answer is no. All souls have been in existence as long as God has, and are not being created as new ones. After all, the soul of each individual exists as an idea of perfect man in the mind of God, which means there are an infinite number of souls in existence as the ideas of God. Some souls have not developed and taken form in some body as yet, but are in the process of developing from the idea to the reality or manifestation. This is one way the expression "new soul" or "young soul" developed, or came into being. No souls are being created as such, but souls are developing from the embryo stage of the idea in God-mind.

(John the Baptist)

Audré, you are very perceptive and stating your questions correctly. First, about John's living in the world, letting his intellectual perception or understanding of spiritual things guide him rather than letting the Father within guide him. He had to decrease or rather, the intellect must give way to the spiritual. You can thus phrase the sentence from the foregoing. Now, to the trait of over-zealousness, which Elijah had not entirely overcome when he attained his Mastership. No master is perfect, but is continually seeking perfection at all times and throughout eternity. To become a Master, one realizes and feels Oneness with the Father within and has mastered the use of his various powers to the extent that is shown in the Bible. Elijah had mastered the art of healing, raising from the dead, and used other powers to produce from substance; such as the widow and the oil. There were other instances also. He still had much to learn and had the tendency of wanting to push others a little faster into understanding their spiritual gifts than they were able to do. This is the over-zealousness of which we speak. I too have certain things to overcome or improve in myself, but we are all doing it.

It is good to discuss the topic about hazards of psychic exploration without adequate safeguards and spiritual assistance. There are some highly developed souls or entities who will help a person, if requested. They will guide an individual from selfish earthbound entities that desire to experience or fulfill certain physical desires through the body of a person on the earth plane. This is the so-called devil or demonic power referred to by many religious leaders, such as Billy Graham.

Now for the prayers with John the Baptist. They are both beautiful prayers. The one I prayed with John reflected both his and my thinking and beliefs. John did not have the full conception of the Father being within as I did. John thought more of going to God than God being within him. We know that he was Elijah incarnated, but John did not realize it at the time. Therefore, I prayed as I did to help John obtain his release from his thinking. Neither of us realized it would be done in the manner it was, nor as quickly. However, it was good for John to be released. Now as Elijah, he has learned through his incarnation as John the Baptist, to be more patient and not to be over-zealous in his activities. In fact, we all learned much through Elijah's action and we are grateful he has grown closer to perfection by his act, which is the goal for all of us.

Printed in the United States
By Bookmasters